Horse Trails in

Arkansas and Oklahoma

Horse Trails in Arkansas and Oklahoma

**Betty Robinson
and
Pat Gordon**

Equestrian Unltd.
Saddlebags Press

London, AR

2004

Address inquiries to:
Equestrian Unltd./Saddlebags Press
PO Box 255, London, AR 72847

Book Design & Photographs by:
Pat Gordon and Betty Robinson

Warning: Some of the trails included in this book may be rugged and remote. As in all outdoor activities there may be dangerous/poisonous creatures and extreme environment to contend with. Although we have made every effort to ensure the accuracy of information in this book, there may be errors and omissions. Because all areas and facilities are evolving, it is possible that some aspects of a trail will be changed after this book has been published.

Trail riding requires the rider to assume responsibility for their own safety. This book is meant to be a guide to established riding areas; a guide to those who already have the requisite experience, and skills to meet the demands of this type of travel. It is the user's responsibility to decide whether they possess the skills and physical fitness required for each ride. The author, publisher and all those association with this publication disclaim any liability for accidents, injuries, damages, or losses that may occur to anyone using this book.

Printed in the United States   *ISBN 0-929183-06-1*

Copies of this book may be purchased from

Saddlebags Press · PO Box 255 · London, Arkansas 72847

Table of Contents

* Indicates a trail included since last publishing.

Acknowledgements

No one writes a book alone, especially a trail book. Consider this...how do you think your favorite trail originated? First it was a huge hunk of forest or grassland or lake shore. Then, someone had a thought, which turned into a dream, which eventually became a plan. With most plans come volunteers. The volunteers often do the grunt work with little or no recognition. Why? Because they are trail riders and they want trails to ride.

After the trails are built how are they maintained? You guessed it. Many are still cared for by volunteers. These people pick up trash left behind by others; they re-hang markers that have been destroyed or torn down; and they worry when there is trail abuse beyond their control. We want to take this opportunity to acknowledge the dreamers, the planners, managing agencies, and all the volunteers that make the trails we all ride today a reality.

Specifically, we want to take this opportunity to thank the people who took their time to offer support or ride with us and share their favorite trail. This list is probably not all inclusive but we tried. If you rode with us and your name isn't listed here, it is an oversight on our part and completely unintentional. We hope the following people will accept our thanks: Jacque Alexander, Audrey Beggs, Rick Bousfield, Gregg Butts, Janet Cantwell, Beth Carr, Linda Collins, Taminia Cooper, Judy Duguid, Mike & Laurel Easton, Asha Erickson, Edianne Erickson, Glenna Ekis, Lee & Cindy Fonkin, Jerry Gilbow, Linda Hybl, Nancy Hawthorne, Edith Jenner, Jim & Sue Joling, Sandy King, Al Knox, Priscilla Kirkpatrick, Randy & Kala Lane, Scott Mashburn, Dave & Becky McMahen, Deanna Olmstead, Dustin Parsons, Leanita Pelts, Alice Singleton, Gloria Stewart, Katie Studdard, Pat Sullivan, Jeanetta Sturgeon, C.E. "Tinker" Tate, Vicki Trimble, Linda White, and Maxine Yeager. We would also like to say thanks to the Arkansas Trail Riders Association, the Oklahoma Equestrian Trail Riders Association, and the Cowgirl Up organization.

Our Support Team. We want to give a special thanks to the people who have worked with us on a daily basis. First, Glenna Ekis, she is our right arm at the farm. The one we turn to when anyone at home needs special care. With her on hand, we never worry. She knows what to do and how to do it. She also gets to ride a trail with us now and then.

Secondly, we want to thank, the farrier, Mack Hayden. Remember the old saying without the foot you have no horse. That idea was never truer than for the trail horse...mule, in this case.

Thank you Mack: for all the care you give the mules; for all the times you juggled your schedule to help us out when we needed to leave early; for all the precision you put into what you do. A mule never lost a shoe because Mack didn't take the extra time when it was necessary.

And last but not least, our thanks to Dr. Shane Parker at the Parker Animal Clinic, in Clarksville, AR. He has never failed to be there when we needed him. When we have been coming in off the trail and had a problem he worked us in. He is always there to consult and advise when it comes to keeping the mules in top shape for the trail.

Thanks to all for what you do to make life on the trail easier.

Introduction

Somewhere deep in our souls we all believe in magic, different kinds of magic maybe, but magic just the same. Trail riders find magic in the sounds of a warm spring morning, the caress of a gentle breeze that cools the sun on our shoulders, or the crispy crunch of bright fall leaves under our horse's hooves. Most of all trail riders believe in the magic of the trail not yet traveled.

Don't misunderstand, we are not ungrateful for the trails we have around home. We love the trails that are tried and true, the friendly ones where each turn is familiar. Those trails provide the substance of our sport, our daily bread. But, many of us have a wanderlust, which was bestowed on us like a legacy from our ancestors. That urge ignites true passion, the challenge to explore and discover. The thrill of the hunt leads us from one trailhead to the next. Each one being special, each one providing surprises and secrets we never considered.

Some of our discoveries are purposely planned while others are simply luck. Being located on an east-west corridor, most people come through both Arkansas and Oklahoma at one time or another. I hear it all the time, "We were on our way through to...and we had heard so many stories about the trails in..., we had to stop". This book invites you to take a closer, more careful look at what you can discover on Arkansas and Oklahoma horse trails.

This book is designed to provide the location of the trails, trailhead, and the nearest services. In addition, you will find a brief description of what you can expect and the overall mileage of the trail system. Most of the time, you also learn what types of facilities to expect at the trailhead.

Horse Trails in Arkansas and Oklahoma

The two states may not claim as many trails as states further west, but the existing trails are exceptional. Slicing Arkansas in half from the northeast to the southwest, most of the horse trails are found in the western half of the state, and almost all of these are in mountainous terrain with an abundance of rock, trees and creek crossing.

In Oklahoma trails are dotted around the state, many are lake trails managed by the US Army Corp of Engineers. These are by their very nature shorter than those you might find in the mountains. Others are managed by State Parks or by the Department of Wildlife. All have their advantages and disadvantages. But the point is, as equestrians looking for places to enjoy our animals we value each and every trail. We devote our spare time to trail advocacy and maintenance. If you want to ride our trails, great, we would love to share, all we ask is that you respect our hard work as much as we do. Leave our trails and our campsites at least as well maintained as you found them.

When you leave camp for the trail, take time to register if is a place to do so. The hikers all register so their numbers tally a high count. Be counted as an equestrian. Let the agencies know we trail riders are using the trails and camps in great numbers. Our economic impact is significant when we stand together. After all, money talks.

Manure monitor: Appoint a designated manure monitor. Before you break camp be sure all manure has been disposed of properly. Each campground or trailhead may have a different policy. Check it out and follow the rules. This makes it much more pleasant for the campers that follow you.

Meeting ATVs: Because some of Arkansas and Oklahoma's best horse trails are multi-use, you run the risk of meeting "four-wheelers". Horses have the right-of-way and almost all of the ATV riders are considerate. They understand their "scare factor" and will readily kill their engines and wait for you to pass. However, what if you are traveling along a specific trail and a group of ATVs overtake your party from behind. It is unfair and inconsiderate for horse riders to continue down the trail at a slow pace and not let the machines pass.

Here is an easy way to solve this dilemma. The horse party should stop and face the ATVers. In a pleasant manner ask the ATVers to shut down their engines. Then all the equestrians ride back past them. This allows the machines to take the lead without scaring anyone out of their wits. Always remember, a thank you goes a long ways to build bridges.

Meeting Bicycles: Horses and mules have the right-of-way, however, this doesn't mean much when your horse has already panicked and dashed into the bushes. Bicycles seem to be an equine's "silent terror". Bikes can be on top of you before you or your animal can hear anything but a swish on gravel. Because the Arkansas trails are so strenuous, bikes riders don't try them often. But if you do meet one, all I can say is good luck. That is one event everyone has to handle in his or her own way.

Other Trail Users: In Arkansas or Oklahoma, unless you get on one of the major hiking trails by mistake, you aren't likely to meet any backpackers. The hikers have enough trails of their own they don't stray onto the multi-use trails. And you will seldom if ever meet a pack string. All the national forests are so full of roads pack strings don't make much sense. The wilderness areas are small and beautiful but most folks just don't spend much time packing in.

Don't cut corners: Think about it! Short cutting across switchbacks encourages erosion. Too much erosion can close a trail. You ride a horse. He does the work. Stay on the trail. If you can't make the whole ride don't go out in the first place or come in early. But don't try to make the ride shorter by cutting corners. You only create an ugly mess and increase problems for everyone. Think low impact.

Bark eaters: Horses and mules are easily bored. Even more than that, some equine just love the taste of tree bark. If your horse or mule is a bark eater please do not tie directly to trees. A bored mule can kill a tree in a few minutes. If you own a tree muncher and must tie to trees once in a while, carry a nosebag and slip it on when you tie up. This solves problems for everyone.

Leave what you find: Many trails are full of artifacts. Almost all trails lead past some old home place, if you know what to look for. However, the most important thing is not, "Do you know what to look for?", but rather, "do you know what to leave behind?" The rule of thumb is don't mess with history. Even the smallest cultural artifacts from previous inhabitants make a difference when piecing together history. Arrowheads, pieces of pottery, grave markers, old foundations and lone rock walls, all tell the story of life, its struggle, and maybe even the death of the previous dwellers. Hopefully, by sharing information and techniques for minimizing the impacts of traveling and camping with horses and mules, our passing will go unnoticed.

§ § §

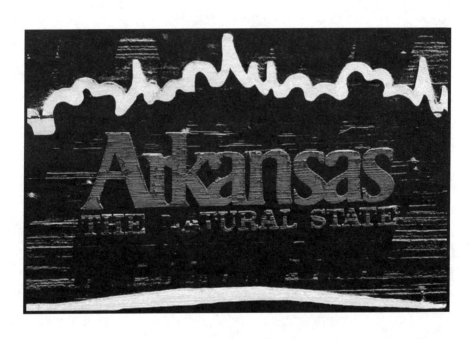

Bear Creek Trails

Distance: 45 miles
Difficulty: Easy to moderate
Fees: None at this time
Type: Public, day-use, overnight camping, multi-use
Facilities: Restroom
Water: Ponds and streams available for horses; no people water
Terrain: Forested setting with some mountains
Trail Markers: Yellow rectangles and Carsonite signs
Trail Maps: Jessieville Ranger District Office
USGS Quadrangle Maps: Steve, Nimrod S.W.

Location
GPS Coordinates: N 34° 47.132' W 093° 09.605'

Bear Creek Horse Trails can be reached by taking Arkansas Highway 7, five miles north of Jessieville, to Forest Service Road 11. Turn West on FR 11, which is a well-maintained gravel road. You will see an auto tour sign pointed in your direction of travel. Continue 4.2 miles on this road to FR 772. Turn right, drive .5 of a mile. You will cross three low water bridges. Camp is on the right.

Description

Trailhead. The trailhead is primitive with five back-in sites. You will find a restroom in the trees near the campsites. Bring your own people-water. During the hottest weather of July and August horse water may be scarce. The camp is near a creek which usually has water year round but in the summer there are no guarantees.

Trails and marking. Bear Creek Horse Trails in the Ouachita Mountains are "user friendly". It is a four loop trail which can cover 45 miles. One of the loops circles the Deckard Walk-In Turkey area and is off limits during turkey season. Significant turns are marked with Carsonite posts. The markers indicate the forest roads you will intersect by following that trail, as well as, the direction of travel. The trails are marked with yellow rectangles. Although you can follow these trails without a map, having one adds pleasure to the ride because it gives you more choices.

The trails consist of forest roads, old logging traces, and narrow wooded trails. The blend is nice and especially good for riders who enjoy a short canter or a chance to shift gears on a gaited horse. The views are good, yet the trail has a lot of shade for hot days. Elevation varies from 800 to 1500 feet.

The trails are multi-use and allow mountain bikes but no ATVs. However, be aware you may meet vehicle traffic on sections of the road.

Nearest Services

Camping and picnic supplies can be found in Jessieville, which is about 11 miles from camp. The nearest veterinary or medical services are in Hot Springs.

For more information:

Jessieville Ranger District
Box 189, 8607 Highway 7 N
Jessieville, AR 71949
501-984-5313
www.fs.fed.us/oonf/ouachita

Blue Mountain Field Trial Area

Distance: Unlimited
Difficulty: Easy
Fees: None
Type: Public, day-use, over-night camping
Facilities: Back-in paved sites with electric; indoor stall; outdoor corrals
Water: Yes, but it has a sulphur taste
Terrain: Grasslands and woods
Trail Markers: None
Trail Maps: None
USGS Quadrangle Maps: Boonville

Location
GPS Coordinates: N 35° 5.116' W 093° 47.041'

From State Hwy 10 in Magazine follow 109 south until it junctions with 217. Turn left on 217 and drive through Sugar Grove. A mile down the road you will find Blue Mountain WLMA on the left.

Description

Trailhead. At the trailhead you have six or so back-in sites with electric. You will find well maintained pipe corrals and a barn with maybe 50 stalls. The indoor stalls have been renovated and many have panels of 3" raw oak. The center stalls are larger and fronted with panel. The side stalls are all standing stalls only. The riding area is accessed from the back of the maintained area.

Trail and marking. The trails are not marked. This is a field trial area maintained for the field trial participants. The area has a network of little used roads and trails. These roads crisscross pastures and wind through open woods. This is a good place to ride if you are comfortable finding your way back to you trailer without the help of markers.

Point of Interest

Field trial events always have first priority. You may not ride while events are in progress. The water in the area has a sulphur taste. If you don't want your horse to go off water, you better haul you own. It usually takes a horse at least two days to be willing to drink the available water. There is a creek nearby that does not smell of sulphur.

Nearest Services

You will find food, fuel, and emergency services in Booneville.

For More Information

Wildlife Management Office
877-525-8606

Brock Creek Multi-Use Trails

Distance: 20 miles to unlimited
Difficulty: Easy to moderate
Fees: None at this time
Type: Public, day-use, and overnight camping
Water: Lake, ponds and streams available for horses
Terrain: Forested setting with some mountain climbs
Trail Markers: Some ribbons
Trail Maps: Yes, Bayou Ranger District Office
USGS Quadrangle Maps: Jerusalem; Cleveland; Lost Corner

Location
GPS Coordinates: N 35° 29.412' W 092°48.011

Take Hwy 124 to Jerusalem, AR, which is northwest of Russellville. In the center of town the highway makes a 90-degree turn. At that junction take County Road 32 north. After a couple of miles, the road number changes because you cross from Conway County to Van Buren County. Follow this road without making any abrupt turns until you come to a small sign on the left which says Brock Lake and points to the right. Turn right and travel down hill maybe three-quarters of a mile. You will come to a Y in the road. To your right is the campground entrance (limited space to turn around). The road you are on leads across the dam. Straight ahead, downhill leads to a second primitive camping area (not recommended for big trailers). Continuing to the far side of the dam you will find plenty of space for even the longest rigs.

Description

Trailhead. If you choose to use the formal campground, remember there is limited space to turn around. Here you will have a restroom, picnic tables and a fire circle. The lower trailhead and the one across the dam are totally primitive.

Trails and marking. A network of trails wind across a valley and several mountain ridges. These trails are pretty much like other Arkansas trails, filled with beautiful scenery and rocks. You will ride up on remnants of several old homesteads. Each discovery is your own and adds to the sense of adventure. Another part of the adventure comes with knowing that at this time these trails are not marked, hopefully, they will be soon.

Tree limbs are low in many places but the trails are easy to see. Remember any time you ride an unmarked trail you run the risk of getting off trail (lost). Good luck and enjoy the trails.

Nearest Services

Services are minimal at Jerusalem, but you can get ice and limited groceries at Appleton. The nearest feed and fuel would be at Adkins. Russellville has the nearest veterinarian and hospital.

For more information

Bayou Ranger District
12000 SR 27
Hector, AR 72843
479-284-3150
www.fs.fed.us/oonf/ozark

Buffalo National River Trails
(three trailheads)

Erbie Horse Camp and Trail

Distance: Cecil Cove Loop, 4 miles
Difficulty: Easy to moderate
Fees: Yes, for overnight camping
Type: Public, day-use, and overnight camping
Facilities: Chemical toilet, picnic tables, fire ring
Water: Pond and river for horses
Terrain: Forested setting; mountainous with some climbing
Trail Markers: Yellow rectangles
Trail Map: Trails Illustrated, Buffalo National River West Half

Location
GPS Coordinates: N 36° 05.723' W 093 16.128'
   Three miles north of Jasper turn left off U.S. Highway 7 at the Erbie Landing sign. For the next eight miles the road twists and turns as it drops toward the Buffalo River. The road is narrow in places with some sharp grades and turns. Pass Erbie Landing on the right, a Ranger's house, the old Clagett Farm and at the old Erbie Church turn left. Keep left following a two-track road into a large open campground. A large tree hangs out over this road that could knock a huge dent in the front of a big trailer. Caution: Big rigs come in on FS19 off of Hwy 7.

Description
   Trailhead. The campground has five sites, with extra parking if necessary. The camp was well maintained at the time of this writing.
   Trails and marking. To find the trail out of camp, look for the Old River Trail signs. This is an out and back trail, which will take you to either Kyles Landing or Pruitt depending on which direction you choose to travel. Cecil Cove Loop is a third alternative. This trail begins at the hiker's parking lot near the restrooms.
   The Cecil Cove Trail begins as a single track. The trees are just far enough apart not to bump your stirrups when you pass.

Yellow rectangles mark the direction. The trail is so well used you really don't have to worry much about markers.

This whole area is steeped in history. Riding up on an old homestead with a house, barn and smoke house is not unusual. Many of the structures are still in good repair. Some are dangerous and show their disintegration. As you ride along the various trails watch for the subtle signs of how the people used to live. You will find rock fences, rock hearths, and chimneys that have not only out lived their people but also the houses that were once built around them. Honor the memory. Leave the artifacts. Besides dragging you backward into the region's history, these features calm your soul and fill your trail ride with top-notch exploring pleasure.

The Cecil Cove Loop dumps out on Erbie Road just above the turn to Farmer's homestead. When the trail meets the road, turn left and keep looking right. As soon as you see a trail, take off in that direction follow it. At the bottom of this short trail is one of the prettiest old homesteads in the loop. On this loop you will also see the Jones Cemetery and Mud Cave.

Nearest Services

Food, feed, and fuel can be found in Jasper. Hospital and veterinarian services are found in nearby Harrison.

For Information:

Upper Buffalo District
HCR 70, Box 366
Jasper, AR 72641
870-446-5373
www.nps.gov/buff

Steel Creek Equestrian Campground

Distance: Unlimited
Difficulty: Easy, moderate, or difficult
Fees: Yes, for overnight camping.
Type: Public, day-use, and overnight camping
Facilities: Chemical toilet, picket poles, picnic tables.
Water: Horse water from the river

Terrain: Forested, river crossings, woods

Trail Markers: In the National River Park marking is kept to a minimum. Trails are usually marked at turns or intersections.

Trail Map: West Half of the Buffalo River Trails Illustrated Map

Location
GPS Coordinates: N 36° 02.404' W 093 20.456'

Take Highway 74 west from Jasper, approximately 11 miles to the small community of Low Gap. At the "Y" stay to the right and continue 2.6 miles. A large archway over a gravel road announces your turn to the right. Shift to 4x4 and go to low gears. This road goes down fast and crooked.

Description

Trailhead. At the bottom, the trailhead is directly to your right. You will find several back-in slots with picnic tables. The trail to Ponca leaves to the south and west through the hikers camping area. The second trail leaves from across the meadow near the bluffs.

Trails and marking. Because this is a National Park, trail markers are slim to none, however the trails are so well used they are fairly easy to follow if you have a map. The Buffalo National River West Half (Trails Illustrated Map) is your best sources of information to find your way around on these trails. From Steel Creek a ride to Ponca and back is about four miles round trip. You will have several river crossings and the opportunity to visit the Villines historical homestead.

To travel the Old River Trail cross the meadow and cross the river, then ride toward Kyles Landing. You have the option of riding out and back or making a loop by riding up the mountain at the old Henderson House to the Center Point Trailhead and then returning to camp.

Point of Interest

Over the years equestrians have had a hard time keeping the right to use the trails in the Buffalo River Area. Please remember riding here is privilege not necessarily a right. Be respectful and help us all continue to enjoy this wonderful slice of history.

Nearest Services

For picnic supplies and gas you can go to Low Gap or Ponca. For diesel you probably have to go to Jasper. Veterinarian and hospital services can be found in Harrison.

For Information:

Upper Buffalo District
HCR 70, Box 366
Jasper, AR 72641
870-446-5373
www.nps.gov/buff

65 Bridge Trailhead

Distance: Unlimited
Difficulty: Easy
Fees: No, this is basically day parking.
Type: Public, day-use.
Facilities: None.
Water: Horse water from river
Terrain: Forested; river crossings, woods
Trail Markers: Yellow rectangles for horses; white rectangles for hikers.
Trail Map: East Half of the Buffalo River (Trails Illustrated) Map

Location
GPS Coordinates: N 35° 59.150' W 092° 44.937'

The Highway 65 Bridge spans the Buffalo River between Silver Hill on the south and St. Joe on the north. Coming from Harrison on the north it's a left immediately before the bridge; from Marshall on the south it's a right turn just after the bridge.

Description

Trailhead. The parking lot is small but will fit 4 or 5 trailers if everyone is considerate when they park.

Trails and marking. This trail is well-trimmed and seems to be used frequently, by both hikers and riders. This is a straight forward trail, follow the yellow rectangles. Watch closely because other trails do branch off this one. The main corridor is marked in yellow. It is approximately 45 minutes to the settlement of Gilbert if you maintain an easy walking pace.

Point of Interest

Gilbert is a small lumber town founded in 1901. A population of 43 to 50 people remain depending on whose figures you use. The old mercantile is still open for business and is more than worth the time to explore. You will find hitching rails and restroom facilities. Riders are asked not to take their horse into town.

The old rail bed down the trail from Gilbert makes an interesting ride. It goes for a mile or so adding to this history and dumps out on a gravel bar where you can enjoy the river and water your horses.

Nearest Services

Gas and food can be found in St. Joe. Veterinary and Hospital services can be found in nearby Harrison.

Information:

National Park Service
Tyler Bend Ranger Office
870-439-2502
www.nps.gov/buff

Burns Park Equestrian Trails

Distance: 8 to 10 miles
Difficulty: Easy
Fees: None
Type: Public, day-use, and overnight camping; multi-use
Facilities: None
Water: Yes, both horse and people
Terrain: Forested setting with bridle paths
Trail Markers: Yellow rectangles and Carsonite signs
Trail Map: None at this time
USGS Quadrangle Maps: North Little Rock

Location
GPS Coordinates: N34° 48.240' W 092° 19.546'

Take I-40 to North Little Rock. Exit at the Burns Park sign. From the west, exit to the right and then turn left back over the Interstate into the park. Directly past the first ballpark, look for Joe Pock Road, which will be a left turn between two buildings. From this point, follow the equestrian trail signs. You will cross back over the interstate. Trail parking is on your right.

Description

Trailhead. The campground is small, maybe ten sites. Some sites are level, while others leave you on a slant. All sites are back-ins. Water is available.

Trails and marking. The trail takes off in both directions from the park. The Yellow trail goes out the backside of camp and hooks up with a fairly wide (seldom used) road. Following this road to the left brings you to a quaint, covered bridge over a small creek. Most riders find this a Kodak moment. You can ride through the bridge, if your animal is willing. If not there is walk across bridge a few yards further on which most horses prefer. The Yellow trail meanders out across some typical Arkansas woods. This loop takes about 45 minutes at a walk. Avoid this area during the rainy season. It's low and boggy.

From the trailer, the red, white, and blue trail starts across the road. The red and blue trail heads up hill while the white trail takes off toward flat land again. The red and blue loop shows they

are 5 and 10 miles long. That may be an over estimate. The red loop runs over the top and hits a black top for a way. Be careful mule shoes are slick on blacktop. In one place you parallel I-40 and the traffic noise is intense. However, this park is a great place to stop and rest if you are traveling cross-country or it is a good place for locals who don't have time to haul on a longer trip. This is also a good place to ride during deer season when the wood aren't safe.

Nearest Services
North Little Rock

For Information
N. Little Rock Parks & Recreation
2700 N. Willow
N. Little Rock, AR 72114
501-753-9312
www.northlittlerock.org/nlrparks/park.html

Byrd Creek Adventure Trails

Distance: Unlimited
Difficulty: Easy to difficult
Fees: Yes, for overnight
Type: Private, day-use, and overnight camping; multi-use
Facilities: Electric, showers and restrooms
Water: Yes, horse and people
Terrain: Wooded; mountainous
Trail Markers: Mostly not marked at this time
Trail Map: None at this time
USGS Quadrangle Maps: Cass; Yale; Ozark

Location
GPS Coordinates: N 35° 40.150' W 093° 44.432'
From I-40 near Ozark, take Hwy 23 north to Cass. Just north of town you will take a right turn and follow Hwy 215, six miles east. Byrd's Adventure Center is on the right.

Description

Trailhead. The trailhead is an open camping area with plenty of room to turn even large rigs around. You will find electric at 80 sites. By the spring of 2005, 40 sites will have water. You will also find hot shower and restrooms
Trails and marking. The trails at this time are scattered over the mountains in the Ozarks. You may follow old logging traces, bike trails, and four-wheeler trails. There is no lack of places to ride, especially if you are capable with a GPS.

Point of Interest
Byrd's Adventure Center is a multi-use private park. You will find all the conveniences like water, electric and showers but you will also run into "jeepers". When you are planning a campout using these facilities, call ahead so you don't run into a crowd.

Nearest Services

Minimal groceries, snacks and ice may be purchased at the camp store. For feed, health care or veterinary services, Ozark is the closest larger town.

For More Information

888-520-7301
www.byrdsadventurecenter.com

Camp Robinson Field Trial Area

Distance: Unlimited
Difficulty: Easy
Fees: None
Type: Public, day-use, and overnight camping
Facilities: Electric, outdoor corrals and stalls under roof.
Water: Yes, people and horse water
Terrain: Flat, grassy, some trees.
Trail Markers: none
Trail Map: None at this time
USGS Quadrangle Maps: Hamlet, Cato

Location
GPS Coordinates: N 34° 57.92' W 092° 20.66'

From I-40, North of Mayflower, take Exit 135 to AR-Hwy 89. Go South on Hwy 89 for 4.2 miles. Turn left on Clinton Road and proceed 2.5 miles. Turn left to WMA Office. Horse camp is past the office area toward the back.

Description

Trailhead. The trailhead is found back of the main office building. Because this is a field trial area you have the opportunity you use box stalls, outdoor corrals, and electric as long as a field trial event is not going on. Field trailers always have priority.

Trails and marking. Covering 25,000 acres of rolling terrain north of Little Rock, Camp Robinson WMA is actually part of the Camp Robinson Military Reservation. The unit closest to Lake Conway is flat and low-lying with young oaks, hickories, sweetgums and cedars. Dense underbrush can make travel difficult for hikers and equestrians. Areas used for riding are open grasslands or two-track roads that network the area. A number of fields are maintained as food plots for wildlife, particularly quail. The best suggestion here is to take a GPS position on camp and then ride where you want to. The area is rider friendly as long as you can find you way back to camp.

Point of Interest

Originally settled by an odd collection of farmers and moonshiners, the area was seized by the US Government before World War I and named Camp Pike. The remaining area was incorporated before WWII to give the installation its present configuration (Arkansas, Bryan Hendricks).

The thick hardwood forest, food plots and gently rolling hills, make this place a favorite of nature buffs including bird watchers, hikers, bikers, and equestrians. The western portion is a Wildlife Demonstration Area maintained for quail hunters to work and train their bird dogs. Field-trailers always have first serve on use.

Nearest Services

Mayflower and Conway.

For Information:

Arkansas Game and Fish Commission
2 Natural Resources Dr.
Little Rock AR 72205
501-223-6300
www.agfc.com

Caney Creek Wilderness Trail

Distance: 16 miles (round-trip)
Difficulty: Easy
Fees: None at this time
Type: Public, day-use, and overnight camping at the west end
Facilities: None
Water: Streams available for horses
Terrain: Forested setting; 15 creek crossing
Trail Markers: The trail is so well used markers are not a
   problem.
Trail Map: District Ranger Office, Mena, AR or
   http://www.fs.fed.us/oonf/rec/caney_map.htm
USGS Quadrangle Maps: Eagle Mountain; Umpire

Location
GPS Coordinates: N 34° 24.583' W 094° 09.926' (west end)

To get to the west trailhead follow Hwy 246, 10 miles out of Vandervoort, which is located on Hwy 71. Turn left on FR 31, go nine miles and turn right to continue on to the trailhead. East trailhead. Take Highway 246 out of Vandervoort 20 miles to FR 38 (the turn off to Shady Lake). Turn left and travel 9.2 miles or just past FR 106 that comes in from Albert Pike Campground. The trailhead is on the left.

Description
Trailheads. The west side has plenty of space for trailers and camping. No facilities.

The east side has enough space for maybe three trailers, unless hikers have filled the parking lot, then you have to park along the road right of way. Horses may be watered in Blaylock Creek, which is within a few feet of the road. The creek may be dry in late summer. The trailhead is best for day rides. This is not a good place to camp overnight.

Trails and marking. This trail runs east to west. Following old road traces and single file trails it makes 15 creek crossings. Riders can stay on the trail and enjoy about a 16 mile round trip or take a topo map and check out your own areas of interest.

The trail is an out-and-back or you have to shuttle your trailer to the other end. Some riders plan to start from each end at the same time, meet in the middle and trade truck keys. This saves time and everyone gets to ride. The trail can also be tied in with the Viles Branch trail for a long ride if you want to shuttle trailers.

The trail in the bottom of the drainage is beautiful and even novice riders should have very little difficulty with the terrain. From the east trailhead Katy Creek crossing is about 4 miles. From this point the trail leads uphill and Buckeye trail junctions to the right. Using this loop you can ride a circle back to the trailers.

The Buckeye Loop IS NOT FOR NOVICE RIDERS. This trail is difficult for even seasoned trail horses and mules. It makes some hard-bottom trail riders suck it up in places. **Ride Buckeye Trail at your own risk**. Another risk on the Buckeye is the plant itself. This plant is listed as poisonous to equine. If your animal is a snatch-and-grabber like mine, one that thinks every trail is a free ticket to the cafeteria—be on guard when you ride this. Many Buckeye leaves are right at temptation height.

Riding this loop clockwise seems to me the less dangerous route. This makes the most dangerous area going up hill, instead of down. When you are going down some of the drops are extreme enough to suggest a dismount. In addition to a couple of challenging drop-offs or upward scrambles depending on your direction, the trees are narrow enough to be real knee knockers. If your animal has any reason to get even for some previous injustice this may be the time.

Buckeye Mountain Trail is a 9-mile trip, which includes a run down a ridge top across the crest of Buckeye Mountain. It is marked with white blazes, and takes off on an old road trace to left about 500 yards up the road from where you parked your trailer at the east trailhead. Views of the entire wilderness are stunning from this ridge, especially during the colder months when there are fewer leaves. Katy Falls between East Hanna and Katy Mountain makes a good lunch spot.

Bring your own water. This wilderness is in constant use. Think low impact. Do not underestimate the ruggedness of the terrain. Treat all water before drinking.

Point of Interest

Caney Creek Wilderness is a 14,433-acre stretch of remote country, which provides the backdrop for a five star horse trail. No motorized vehicles are allowed. The only way to see this remote beauty is by horse, mule or on foot. The area is filled with huge oaks, beeches and pines. In the spring wildflowers spread all the colors of the rainbow in blankets across the meadows.

Nearest Services

Food, fuel, and feed can be found in Mena or Glenwood.

For More Information

District Ranger
Route 3, Box 220, Hwy. 71 N
Mena, AR 71953
870-394-2382
www.agfc.com/wma_lakes/wma_caney_creek.html
www.southernregion.fs.fed.us/ouachita/recreation/trails/caneyc
reek.shtml

Devil's Den Horse Camp & Trails

Distance: 25 miles plus
Difficulty: Moderate to difficult
Fees: Yes, for overnight
Type: Public, day-use, and overnight camping
Facilities: 40 sites, electric, water, hot showers and restrooms
  All sites are reservable. Call for reservations.
Water: Yes, both horse and people
Terrain: Forested setting with some steep climbs.
Trail Markers: Colored diamonds designates each trail
Trail Map: Devil's Den State Park Office
USGS Quadrangle Maps: Rudy NE, Strickler, Winslow

Location
GPS coordinates: N 35° 46.376' W094° 15.845'

To reach the Devil's Den Horse Camp, travel eight miles south of Fayetteville on I-540 to Exit # 53 (West Fork), then go 17 miles southwest on State Hwy 170; or you may take exit #45 (Winslow) and go 7 miles east on State Hwy 74. TRAILERS LONGER THAN 26 FT. SHOULD TAKE EXIT #53 AND DRIVE Hwy 170 TO THE HORSE PARK. HWY 74 HAS STEEP SWITCHBACKS THAT CAN BE A PROBLEM WHEN USING LONG TRAILERS.

If you approach the park from Hwy 170 you will see the equestrian camp sign before you go completely down into the park. The sign will be on your right and it will be a right turn. The road turns from blacktop to gravel. The horse camp will be on the left. If you approach Devil's Den Park from Hwy 74, you will pass the office and continue down hill. Stay on the blacktop, cross the bridge and proceed up hill. The sign will be on your left, turn left and follow the road to camp, which will be on the left.

Description

Trailhead. The horse camp lays in a circle with plenty of shade. Almost all sites are back-in and may be reserved. Water is available at most sites. A restroom with hot showers is located near the entrance.

Trails and marking. You have access to three trails from the horse camp. All are color coded.

Old Road Trail (4 ½ miles long) is blazed in yellow and begins across the from the horse camp entrance. Near the edge of a small clearing, a marked trail leads up the mountain. Although the beginning incline seems rather steep, climbing some 800 feet, the Old Road Trail is rated as easy in comparison to the Red and Green loops.

Although this loop trail can be traveled in either direction, most choose to ride clockwise. Going left at the fork, the trail gradually ascends the hill often following an old CCC road and finally crossing Hwy 170. All riders should use caution when crossing the highway.

After crossing, the trail descends to a junction with the Yellow Rock hiking trail. While horses are not allowed on foot trails, you may wish to tie up and walk the short distance to a bluff that looms 250 feet over Lee Creek Valley. The horse trail follows the bench, working its way around the mountain and under the CCC overlook. After a second highway crossing it loops back to the main trail. Take a left and you are on your way back to camp.

Holt Ridge Trail (7 miles long) blazed in red, and the **Vista Point Trail** (9 miles long) blazed in green, both begin inside the horse camp near the bathhouse. Note: Both of these trails venture into the adjoining Ozark National Forest. Because the Devil's Den Trail system is the oldest permanently marked horse trail in Arkansas, many sections have seen some hard use. In places you need to watch your horses' footing because prominently exposed tree roots and large rock can be dangerous.

As the trail leaves camp and proceeds down Lee Creek it passes one of the three natural bridges that can be seen on the trip. On the long gradual climb to Holt Ridge, riders travel around the perimeter of the maintenance compound, and ride within view of Hwy. 74. These two trails are difficult enough that it would be helpful for either the horse or rider to have some trail experience. The terrain is steep and rocky.

Vista Point Trail passes above Blackburn Creek. Expect some steep climbs and ledge riding. This trail, if followed in it's entirety, is not recommended for novice riders. Following the jeep road to the right at an intersection near Hwy 74, riders pass the site of the Old Mt. Olive School and Church which served the homesteaders in this area from 1880 to 1937.

Vista Point Overlook offers one of the finest views into the rugged wilderness of the Boston Mountains. A hundred yards beyond the overlook, the horse trail joins the Butterfield hiking trail for a short distance. Once the riders leave the bluff edge, the trail passes through the lower CCC quarry or drops down a steep incline to follow the bench. The quarry provided sandstone boulders for the park's cabins, restaurant, and visitor center. The trail crosses the ridge and rejoins the Holt Road Trail. Follow the blaze to the right or northeast, to reach the overlook and complete the loop. At the trail junction, you may follow the blazes to the left down the ridge, across the creek and back to the horse camp or you may stay on top and follow the red diamonds along the bluff and return by crossing Lee Creek farther west.

Point of Interest

The rugged terrain of the Ozark Mountains provides the backdrop for 2200 acres of spectacular scenery. The caves, canyons and crevices add intrigue to the natural wonders that surround you.

History books describe this section of Arkansas as "the dreaded range of the Boston Mountains". When the Butterfield Overland Stage operated through this territory, it required a four-mule hitch of the best animals available to navigate the steep terrain.

Legend claims the Devil's Den Cave as a rendezvous site for notorious outlaws who roamed the turbulent country in the early 1800's. The Civilian Conservation Corp developed the park for visitors and established trails. The cave extends 550 feet into the mountain. Flashlights are needed for exploration.

Devil's Den State Park offers a variety of services for your enjoyment. Sixteen fully equipped cabins, which includes kitchen, fireplace and air conditioning, makes the visit a pleasure for those who choose not to stay in the horse camp, although horses are not allowed in this area. A restaurant, gift shop, and store are open through the summer. A swimming pool is available for family enjoyment, as well as, paddle boats, canoes and a playground. Rent-a-Backpack units are available for visitors who would like to camp or backpack, but don't have the necessary equipment. Mountain bike and hiking trails are provided in addition to the horse trails.

The Visitor Center houses an interpretive exhibit area, audiovisual room and park offices. Interpretive services are provided year-round. In this park you can find something for the entire family.

Horses are not permitted on park roads or in camping areas other than the horse camp. Horses are not permitted on any foot trails with the exception of the short stretch where the Butterfield Hiking Trail and the horse trail overlap. You may meet hikers or bikers. Be prepared. Bikers and hikers should yield to horses.

Nearest Services

Food, ice, and picnic supplies can be found at the park store. A restaurant and gift shop is open from Memorial Day through Labor Day. Gas and other conveniences are located at Winslow or West Fork. Medical and veterinary services are available in Fayetteville.

For Information:

Devil's Den State Park
11333 West AR Hwy 74
West Fork, AR 72774
479-761-3325
devilsden@arkansas.com
www.ArkansasStateParks.com

Eight West Equestrian Trail

Distance: 29.5 (perimeter trail)
Difficulty: Easy
Fees: None at this time
Type: Public, day-use
Facilities: None
Water: Streams available for horses
Terrain: Forested setting; some mountainous with a few climbs
Trail Markers: Blazes on trees; Carsonite markers at turns
Trail Map: Mena Ranger District Office
USGS Quadrangle Maps: Mountain Fork, Rich Mountain, Potter, Mena

Location
GPS coordinates: N 34° 37.100' W 094° 18.332
   Follow Hwy 8 West from U.S. 71 in Mena, four miles to Peach Orchard Road which is now County Road 41. This road is marked with a blue and yellow sign which is difficult to see from your direction of travel. Turn right. Continue until you cross a cattle guard. At this point do not turn left, that is private drive. Continue across a second cattle guard and you will see a large tree and a brown gate. You can park in any wide spot along the road, but most equestrians park here because of the room to unload.

Description

Trailhead. There are no facilities at this trailhead or anywhere along this trail. You may water from streams or ponds when you find them. Parking is primitive and minimal.

Trails and marking. Ride through the gate. Be sure to close it behind you. This is a farmer's pasture. Please be respectful. Being observant helps protect all users' rights to ride. Markers are yellow and orange blazes on trees. Some older markings, green and yellow horseshoes, are still visible.

On the western portion of this trail you ride for about 5.4 miles on a wide trail that twists across the crest of Self Mountain. The Forest Service advertises the trail as dry but we found some water at various spots most of the year. You will see a variety of vistas and old rock fences. This is an easy trail as far as riding skill required. The trail is constructed of a number of loops. You can create a ride as long or short as you desire.

Markings are not abundant particularly on the lower portion of loop six which is the west loop. Although, these trails are used by four-wheelers, as well as, equestrians, they don't receive major use by anyone. If you are looking for a good place to take a day off with an equine friend, this is a good place to do it.

Point of Interest

In southwestern Arkansas, you will find Polk County snug against the Oklahoma border. The landscape is picturesque and remote. Most of the early towns developed with the railroad, which marched across the country in 1896 One of the most infamous men to inhabit these mountains was Little George Hensley. Being a mountain survivalist, Little George evaded lawmen for 34 years. He supported himself by being a self-employed bounty hunter, robbing banks, and running moonshine.

"Outlawing was hard and dangerous work in the early 1900's. Little George did make some good heists in his bank-robbing career, but easy come easy go. In Cogburn folklore Little George will always be remembered as the Robin Hood of the Ouachita Mountains." *(Looking Glass Magazine).*

Stories such as these add to the mystique of riding the remote horse trails that have been chiseled from the rugged mountain terrain.

Nearest Services

Food, fuel, feed, health and veterinary services can be found in Mena.

For More Information

Mena Ranger District
Rt. 3, Box 220
U.S. Highway 71
870-394-2382
www.fs.fed.us/oonf/ouachita

Fourche Mountain Horse Trails

Distance: 27
Difficulty: Easy; moderate; difficult
Fees: None at this time
Type: Public, day-use, and overnight camping
Facilities: None
Water: Streams available for horses
Terrain: Forested setting; some mountainous with some tough climbs
Trail Markers: Yellow rectangles on trees, additional yellow arrows at turns, some Carsonite markers
Trail Map: Poteau Ranger District Office, Waldron
USGS Quadrangle Maps: Waldron S, Y-City, Parks, Oden

Location
GPS coordinates: N 34° 43.594' W 093° 59.434'
Five miles east of Y-City. Parking for trailhead is on the south side of U.S. 270 across from Mill Creek Recreation Area. You may also camp at the Mill Creek Recreation Campground in the equestrian section, when you can find it open.

Description
Trailhead. There are no facilities at either site. The trailhead across the road from Mill Creek Campground is probably the best. You have a large pasture to park in. You may use portable corrals or tie to your trailer.

Trails and marking. The trails are clearly marked with yellow rectangular blazes. Most turns have an additional yellow arrow indicating the direction of the turn. Carsonite markers are placed at significant points with numbers so you can tell by looking at the map exactly where you are. Mileage has been added to the maps so you can figure you distance from camp.

The Fourche Mountain Trail offers great views of Fourche Mountain and Buck Knob. The higher elevation, especially between point 4 and 5 are extremely rough and have little water. The outside perimeter of the trail will take you most of a day.

Point of Interest

On this trail you will find the remnants of an old silver mine, a civil war entrenchment area and not far from the upper loop, you can still find the remains of a WWII plane crash. These trails give you a good concept of the nature of the Ouachita Mountains.

Nearest Services

Food and fuel at Y- City; feed, health care and veterinarian services in Mena.

For More Information

Poteau Ranger District
P.O. Box 100
Waldron, AR 72858
870-637-4174
www.fs.fed.us/oonf/ouachita

Hobbs State Park Equestrian Trail

Distance: 17 miles at the time of publishing
Difficulty: Moderate
Fees: Check with management
Type: Public, day-use, and possible overnight with permission
Facilities: Level parking pads with access to horse water
Water: Stream available for horses; no people water in parking area.

Terrain: Ridges, hills, woods, and some climbs
Trail Markers: None at the time of publishing
Trail Map: Check with Hobbs State Park Office
USGS Quadrangle Maps: War Eagle

Location
GPS Coordinates: N 36° 16.323' W 093° 57.048'
Take Hwy 12 out of Rogers to War Eagle Mill. You will see directions to the equestrian area.

Description
The 11,644 acres is typical Ozark Mountain terrain. The trail winds across ridges speckled with hardwoods and shortleaf pine. Beaver Lake lies on the northern boundary and War Eagle Creek

defines the southern one. Formerly known as Beaver Lake State Park, now known as Hobbs State Park-Conservation Area, it is in the initial stages of development at the time of this writing. I have had the opportunity to ride these trails and they will be a fun ride when finished. If you are curious and ready to ride these trails, call management for specific details. They are due to open in November or December of 2004.

Point of Interest

Hobbs State Park-Conservation Area is jointly managed by Arkansas State Parks, the Arkansas Natural Heritage Commission and the Arkansas Game and Fish Commission. A pre-Civil War historic area, containing an important industrial site and slave quarters, is located in Van Winkle Hollow. The cultural and historical significance of this site ranks highly both in northwest Arkansas and across the state. Hitching rails are planned so the history will be more easily accessible by foot for equestrians because horses are not allowed in that area. The trailhead and trail marking were in progress at the time of publication.

Nearest Services

Beans, cornbread, sandwiches, and cobbler are available from the Bean Palace Restaurant located in the War Eagle Mill, which is open during spring, summer, and fall. Other eating establishments are located around the lake. Fuel can be found on Hwy 412 coming out of Springdale. Hospital and veterinary services are available from either in Rogers, Springdale, or Fayetteville.

For More Information

Hobbs State Park-Conservation Area
20344 E. Hwy 12
Rogers, AR 72756
1-479-789-2380
www.agfc.com/wma_lakes_wma_hobbs.html

Huckleberry Mountain Horse Trails

Distance: 34 miles of marked FS trails. Other trails are marked in the area.

Difficulty: Easy, moderate, difficult

Fees: $3.00 day-use from Sorghum Hollow Campground; none if you use other locations. $5.00 a day if you park at Lonesome D campground

Type: Public, day-use, and overnight camping

Facilities: Chemical toilets, fire rings, picnic tables

Water: Ponds and streams crossings

Terrain: Forested setting, mountainous, several steep climbs

Trailheads: Three

Trail Markers: Blazes on trees, Carsonite markers at turns

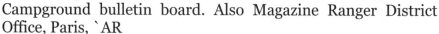

Trail Maps: Often available at Sorghum Hollow Campground bulletin board. Also Magazine Ranger District Office, Paris, `AR

USGS Quadrangle Maps: Scranton; Chickalah Mt. West; Magazine Mt. NE; New Blaine

Location
GPS coordinates:
#1 Sorghum Hollow Camp **N 35° 15.367 W 093° 28.194'**
#2 Huckleberry Camp **N 35° 14.925 W 093° 28.900'**
#3 Magazine Mountain **N 35° 10.565 W 093° 35.711'**
#4 Lonesome D **N 35° 16.650' W 093 29.603'**

You can access Lonesome D, Sorghum Hollow, and Huckleberry Camp from Hwy 22 between Midway and New Blaine.

Description

Trailheads.

Sorghum Hollow Camp can be accessed .5 of a mile east from the junction of U.S. 22 and 64. Turn on Sorghum Hollow Road (FR1614) and travel 4.7 miles to the camp on the left. This developed campground has 15 primitive campsites and a vault toilet. Campsites are large and open with plenty of room for large rigs and horse water is available from a nice pond.

Huckleberry Camp is 11 miles south of Paris. Travel on Hwy 309 to FR 1601. Turn left and continue 8 miles. Follow FR 1601 across Millard Ford, and past Liberty School. One mile beyond the Mt. Grove/Rogers cemetery turn left on FR 1613 and proceed 3.5 miles to camp, the road actually dead ends at the camp. Horse water from lake. No other facilities.

Mt. Magazine Camp is 16.2 miles from Paris on Scenic Byway 309. You will find a small sign. Camp is on the right. This location is capable of holding a ton of trailers. No water except what you can take out of the rock quarry by bucket. Care should be taken if you lead your horse to water. Remember rock quarries notoriously have no bottom. Don't let you horse try to walk into the water.

Lonesome D Camp is privately owned. From Dardanelle follow Hwy 22, 18.5 miles. From New Blaine it is 3.5 miles. You will see a red sign on you left. From Midway on Hwy 22 it is approximately 3 miles before you turn right. The road is Cravens Lane. It is one mile to camp. You will cross one low water bridge and take a right. The road can be rough. Camp has water, electric, toilet, showers, and corrals.

Trails and marking. From Mount Magazine camp the yellow trail travels down the south side of the mountain at about an 8% grade. Remember what goes down must come back up so be aware of your horse's condition. You will find a tough pull back into this campsite. On this trail you cross Highway 309 and pass the Old Apple place. Once you are at the bottom you cross Millard Ford where you can pick up the orange trail or continue on along the yellow.

Riding the trail clockwise after you cross Millard Ford, you will follow Big Shoal Creek, crossing it several times. Once you are in the Big Shoal Creek drainage you have the option of several trails. The FS trail that winds Huckleberry Mountain brings you to the Huckleberry Campground at a lake where you can water your mount. Taking other trails marked with ribbons will bring you to Lonesome D Campground.

When you are on top of Huckleberry you have two options. One is to take the loop marked on the top which is also the Walk-in Turkey area, you will pass Bell Springs and have some beautiful panoramic views of the Arkansas River Valley. From the top of Huckleberry you can see seven towns and the Nuclear Power Plant at London, Arkansas.

The second option is to follow the markers down a steep jeep trail to a bench trail. Here you choose to go back toward Shoal Creek or continue on down to Sorghum Hollow campground. Be sure to pick up a forest service map and this will all make more sense.

Organized rides of 25 or more must have a special-use permit. This is a multi-use trail. Camping is permitted along the trail, but is subject to general forest regulations. Scatter hay and manure when camping in the forest. From April to May, a portion of the orange trail is closed for turkey hunting and nesting season. Contact the District Office for specific dates and location.

Point of Interest
The bulk of the territory covered by the thirty-four miles of permanent horse trails in the Mt. Magazine trail system lays in Logan country. Pine Ridge, which is north of and parallel to Huckleberry, Rich and Magazine mountains separates Sorghum Hollow from the modern world as it has throughout history.

Twenty-four families once called the five or six square miles home between Little Bigger Creek on the east and Big Shoal Creek on the west. Now the horse trail meanders around trees, which grow in the center of old wagon tracks. The trail travels past moss covered rock piles, which remind you where homesteads once stood. Crumbling rock chimneys leave silent images of where families worked and played.

Legends made of fact and fiction pass from one generation to another. Huckleberry Mountain Horse Trail area has its share of such folklore. A buried treasure legend tells of gold and silver buried by de Soto and his men. The story claims the Spanish conquistadors made a swing through the beginning of the Ozark Mountains crossing the Arkansas River at Dardanelle. The Spaniards, leading several mules packed with gold and silver, were pursued by a band of hostile Indians. To travel faster the Spaniards placed the treasure under a bluff on a ridge of Rich Mountain and blasted the cliff down to bury the treasure. Fact or fiction, the legend survives. You can still ride to this area and find the unsuccessful excavation work done by zealous treasure hunters.

Folklore of Bushwhacker Bluff is rooted in the Arkansas history of the Civil War. During the period of 1861-65 evaders and deserters roamed the Ozark Mountains. Many bushwhackers and guerrillas looted and pillaged the unprotected homes in the Magazine area. These renegades knew the price for their cruel ways would be high when the homeowners returned from the war. Hearing the rumor that a group of soldiers were returning, the desperados planned to shoot the soldiers as they passed along the road below Needles Eye Cave. However, one of the returning soldiers learned of the ambush from a protective relative. Being forewarned, the soldiers took the outlaws by surprise and forced the outlaws to jump off the bluff. When you ride through the picturesque woods, it is easy to feel you have returned through time to those days when the Civil War was ending.

Millard Ford is in the lower part of Bear Hollow, where the main road crosses Big Shoal Creek. The small hamlet of Millard supported a gristmill, cotton gin, store, and post office. The little town was a crossroads for horse, oxen and wagon travel. All that's left of this once booming village is a millstone turned on its side a few yards upstream from the crossing.

Nearest Services

Food, fuel, feed, health and veterinary services can be found in Paris. Food and fuel are in Midway and New Blaine.

For Information:
Mt. Magazine Ranger District
P. O. Box 511
Paris, AR 72687
479-963-3076
www.fs.fed.us/oonf/ozarks

Lonesome D Equestrian Trails

Distance: A variety of loops. Make it as long as you want
Difficulty: Easy, moderate, difficult
Fees: $5.00 a day per trailer, overnight camping fee varies with
services
Type: Private camping, public trails
Facilities: Hot shower, flush toilets, corrals, RV hookups
Water: Available at each campsite and on the trail.
Terrain: Forested setting, mountainous with many climbs,
vistas, and creek crossings
Trail Markers: Ribbons, painted horseshoes on trees, blazes,
Carsonite markers
Trail Map: Check with campground office
USGS Quadrangle Maps: Scranton; Chickalah Mt. West;
Magazine Mt. NE; New Blaine

Location
GPS Coordinates: N 35° 16.645' W 093 29.575'

From Dardanelle follow Hwy 22 west, 18.5 miles. From the
sign at New Blaine Park 3.5 miles to left turn. You will see a
Lonesome D sign on the left. This is Cravens Lane. From here it
is one mile to camp. If you are coming from Midway it is
approximately 3 miles on your right turn.
Cross one low water bridge and make a right, you can't miss it.

Description
Trailhead. You will find 35 modern sites. Two have electric,
water, and sewer. All the rest have electric and water. There is a
dump site on your way out.
Trails and marking. Riders may access trails several ways. If
you leave by the old logging road it is wide enough to ride stirrup
to stirrup. Or you may take a winding trail near a creek. Or leave
from the back and head right up one of the ridges. Each route has
its own beauty and leads to new and exciting discoveries. Many
of the Lonesome D trails hook up with Huckleberry Forest
Service Trails.

You will find trails to two different cafes. Both make great hamburgers and have cold sodas. If you worry about getting lost, camp management will help you find a guide.

Although you may find some 4-wheelers and mountain bikes the major user of these trails are equestrian. You may camp along the trail subject to forest regulations. Be aware high water levels can make crossing Shoal Creek dangerous. The crossings are easily negotiated during normal weather.

Nearest Services
Ice and farrier are provided in camp. Other supplies may be purchased at Midway or New Blaine. Nearest large towns are Paris (to the west) and Dardanelle (to the east).

For Information
Lonesome D Horse Camp
776 Cravens Lane
New Blaine, AR 72851
479-938-2899 or 479-938-0149
www.lonesomed.com

Madison County WLMA Trails

Distance: 45 plus miles
Difficulty: Easy, moderate, difficult
Fees: None at this time
Type: Public, day-use, and over-night camping
Facilities: None
Water: Streams for horses; no people water
Terrain: Mountainous; rocky, woods, big pine, hickory and
    walnut trees
Trail Markers: Jar lids nailed on trees, red, yellow, and blue
Trail Maps: Yes, from Internet
USGS Quadrangle Maps: Forum; Rock house

Location
GPS Coordinates: N36°12.556' W 093° 42.025'
From Huntsville (southeast of Fayetteville), take Hwy 23 north approximately 12 miles. Directional signs indicate access roads from Hwy 23 to the interior of the area. Maps indicate camp locations.

The above coordinates will take you to campsites 1 through 4. Twenty-three primitive sites exist.

Description
Trailhead. In this area the trailhead is wherever you choose to park. You will need a map, some local help, or good luck the first time you ride here. It is a wonderful, challenging, and  beautiful place to ride but the trails are kept low profile. At most campsites you will find plenty of room for even large trailers. If you look carefully you will find campsites close to cool fresh spring water for the horses. Some of the higher camps have only pond water and you may have to walk 50 yards or so.

Trails and marking. Trails are marked with painted circles from canning jar lids. Three trails with three different colors. Two of the favorite places to go are Kettle Cave and the King River overlook. Both are great. The general riding atmosphere is mountainous and woods.

Point of Interest

This area is designated for hunting. When hunting seasons are in progress equestrians may not use the area. This begins October 1 and goes through the end of January. To know for sure about riding, check with management before you pull there.

Nearest Services

Food, feed, and emergency services can be found in Huntsville or Eureka Springs.

For More Information

877-967-7577
www.agfc.com/wma_lakes/wma_madison_county.html

Mill Creek Trails

Distance: 27 miles of perimeter trail; 15 miles of interior loops
Difficulty: Moderate to difficult
Fees: None
Type: Public, day-use, and overnight camping
Facilities: One chemical toilet
Water: Stream for horses and mules
Terrain: Mountainous; several stream crossings
Trail Markers: Blue plastic diamonds and blue marks on trees
for outside loop. Inside loops are orange, yellow, and white.
Trail Maps: Yes, contact Boston Mountain Ranger District
Office or
www.fs.fed.us.oonf/ozark/recreation/rogs/mill_creek.html
USGS Quadrangle Maps: St. Paul; Cass

Location
GPS Coordinates: N 35° 45.796' W 093° 51.628
Mill Creek trailhead is located near Combs, AR, off Hwy 16.
Turn south at the Mill Creek bridge on FS Road 1007 for 4 miles;
turn left on FS Road 1509, go ½ mile to the trail head.

Description
Trailhead. The trailhead is large with room for several trailers.
You will find one vault toilet and a bulletin board with
information about the area. Do not count on finding individual
maps at the bulletin board. There is room to park on both sides
of the road and both sides of Mill Creek near the road.

Trails and marking. The perimeter trail is marked in blue
either with diamonds or blazes painted on trees. The length is
close to 27 miles if you stay to the outer trail. The inner loops are
marked with different colors: orange, yellow, and white. This is a
multi-use trail. Expect ATVs and mountain bikes. The trail
traverses remote areas of the Ozark National Forest and features
some spectacular terrain. But the problem is, the trail was truly
laid out for ATVs. Almost all trails going to the top or the bottom
of the mountains go either straight up with short bench stops or
straight down. This is fine for hard pulling engines but it is
difficult for horses and really not that much fun for the rider

either. This is a trail each rider would have to ride once and make their own decisions. Is the scenery worth the effort?

Point of Interest

Several rock walls decorate the trail sides. You will also cross a wonderful clear creek. Choose the middle of the week to ride this trail and you will have less ATV traffic.

Nearest Services

The nearest town for all services would be Fayetteville. You can find most everything you need in Elkins or Huntsville.

For More Information

Boston Mountain Ranger District
P.O. Box 76
Hwy. 23
Ozark, AR 72949
479-667-2191

Moccasin Gap Trails

Distance: Perimeter loop 28 miles
Difficulty: Easy, moderate, difficult
Fees: $3.00
Type: Public, day-use, and overnight camping
Facilities: 17 camp sites, chemical toilets, water, and pavilion
Water: Yes, people and horse water in the center of campground
Terrain: Forested setting, mountainous with many climbs, vistas, and creek crossings
Trail Markers: Markers at turns and colored triangles on trees
Trail Maps: Moccasin Gap Trailhead: Mack's Pines; Bayou Ranger District Office, Hector, AR
USGS Quadrangle Maps: Simpson; Treat NE; Smyrna NW; Treat SE

Location
GPS Coordinates: N 35° 34.426' W 093° 04.133'

(Private Campground Mack's Pines N 35° 33.291 W 093° 04.765)

Twenty-one miles north of I-40 on Scenic Highway 7 out of Russellville.

Description

Trailhead. The campsite is large and you will find easy access even for large trailers, however, all sites are back-in.

Trails and marking. The trail system forms a series of loops with varying degrees of difficulty based on steepness, trail surface, and the number of creek crossings. The loops are named for the area through which they pass. Trails are marked by color-coded symbols on trees. Junctions are marked with letters on round white posts. Trails are marked in both directions. Connector trails are marked in the color towards which you are riding. The symbols vary in color according to the loop.

Stave Mill Falls Loop (red circles) You can ride the red loop as an access route to any of the other trails. The red loop is the closest loop to camp. Stave Mill Falls, which is a very scenic area, is located approximately 2 miles from camp. Although the falls run most of the year, in dry years it may be hard to locate. The trail crosses over the top of the falls, traversing the creek on a short section of slab rock. Even though there is a steep hill on this loop, it remains the favorite for many riders.

Black Oak Ridge Loop (pink diamonds) The pink trail runs along a ridge above Moccasin Hollow. The trail consists of two meandering elongated circles. It is well marked and well trimmed. From the first pink loop you have access to Mack's Pines for cold drinks and snacks.

Gap Hollow Loop (blue triangles) This is a combination of logging roads and two-track trails. This is also the closest connection to the High Mountain Loop from the horse camp. The trail is shady even in mid-afternoon. The trail skirts the edge of a deep hollow and, except during the wet season, will be a dry ride.

High Mountain Loop (yellow circles) Even on sunny days most sections of this loop are in the shade. High Mountain Loop is a series of loops that make the trail quite long. Portions of this trail are rugged and are not recommended for the novice rider or inexperienced horse. You will find some very steep climbs and downhills, a breast collar and crupper are recommended. If you do not have either you may need to stop and readjust your saddle at the top or the bottom. Horses unfamiliar with hills will often start bucking when the saddle goes forward over their withers or scoots back out of position.

If you ride here during spring or fall hunting season, be sure to wear hunter orange. Roads that are unmarked are not part of the trail system. There are no rules against riding on them but you take you own chances about getting lost. Scatter manure and hay before leaving horse camp. Please do not make shortcuts on trails or cut switchbacks. This does tremendous damage to trails.

This is a popular trail for mountain bikes, dirt bikes, 4-wheelers, and equestrians. We must all do our part to get along with other user groups and protect the trails. Be courteous.

For Information
Bayou District Ranger
Rt. 1 Box 36
Hector, AR 72843
479-284-3150
www.fs.fed.us/oonf/ozarks

Pea Ridge National Military Park Equestrian Trail

Distance: 14 miles
Difficulty: Easy
Fees: None at this time
Type: Day-use
Facilities: None
Water: None
Terrain: Flat and basically open
Trail Markers: Permanent metal markers
Trail Maps: Check with visitor's center
USGS Quadrangle Maps: Bentonville North; Pearidge

Location
GPS Coordinates: N 36° 26.643 W 094 1.657'

Driving U.S. 62 north from Rogers, the first sign you see announces a turn to the town of Pea Ridge. Do not turn there; continue on until you see the entrance to the Pea Ridge National Battlefield on the left. Turn here, drive past the Visitors Center and through the parking lot. Continue straight ahead to the point where the car tour for the battleground begins, at this point you will see a gravel road leading into a hay meadow. There are two large trees for shade and ample space for trailers. This is the designated horse parking area.

Description

Trailhead. There are no facilities for man nor beast at this park. The trailhead is open with plenty of room for trailers.

You will find restrooms and people drinking water in the Visitor's Center, which is within walking distance from the equestrian area. Exhibits of Civil War artifacts such as muskets, cannons and uniforms, as well as, a 12-minute visual presentation can add interest to your ride.

Trails and marking. The trails consist of rolling hills on shaded paths. The paths are mowed frequently so they stay open. The beginning of the trail is excellent for cantering. This is a good trail for the novice horse and rider. It is mostly flat with good footing. The last part of the trail, which crosses Pea Ridge, is a little rocky. The trail forms a large irregular circle, which encompasses most of the legendary bloody battlefield. The horse trail stays away from the main points of interest however, it does pass close enough for you to see the old Tavern, although you are not allowed to ride up to it.

During the dry season you will not find water on the trail. Some sections show signs of being boggy in wet weather. Check in at the visitor's center. Let people know you are using the trail. We need the support. This is also a good trail to ride during deer gun season because no hunting is allowed in the park.

Point of Interest

Pea Ridge National Military Park, consists of 4,210 acres containing essentially all the land over which brothers, sons, and fathers from the North and South fought the battle of Pea Ridge on March 7 and 8, 1862.

This National Military Park is the backdrop for a decisive victory for Union forces. The theater held a bitter, bloody two-day battle in which Federal Army Commander Brig. Gen. Samuel R. Curtis defeated the Confederate Command of Gen. Earl Van Dorn. Two confederate Generals, Ben McCullough, and James McIntosh were killed during the siege. As a result of this battle, the Confederates were never again in control of the Ozarks Hills. Additionally, the Cherokee Indians changed their allegiance from the South to the North.

The only visible evidence of the battle is the Federal Trenches in the single detached section of the park on the bluffs of the Little Sugar Creek. The battle fought here is known by two names "The Battle of Elkhorn Tavern" or "The Battle of Pea Ridge". Elkhorn Tavern is the most famous historical landmark that remains. The first structure was not built as a tavern but as a private home. The building became the center for community activity, serving as a trading post, post office and a place of worship.

The route of the Butterfield Overland Stage passed this tavern. Folks stopped for refreshments and some stayed over. The tavern was actually named for the large elk horn and skull that was placed on the ridge-pole. These famous horns still remain there.

Nearest Services

Food, feed, and fuel may be found in Rogers.

For Information

Pea Ridge National Military Park
Park Superintendent
Pea Ridge, AR 72751
www.nps.gov/peri/

Sugar Creek Equestrian Trails

Distance: 35 miles
Difficulty: Easy to moderate
Fees: None at this time
Type: Public, day-use, and overnight camping; multi-use
Facilities: None
Water: Ponds and streams available for horses
Terrain: Forested setting with some mountains
Trail Markers: Yellow rectangles and yellow on posts
Trail Maps: Cold Springs Ranger District Office
USGS Quadrangle Maps: Sugar Grove

Location
GPS Coordinates: N 35° 1.001 W 093° 52.008'

From State Highway 23 southeast of Ft. Smith take Highway 116 East to County Road 19. Turn south for 8 miles to Knopper's Ford Recreation Area. Go south past Knopper's Ford ½ mile to Road S30. Turn left. Go approximately ½ mile to horse trail parking and camping area.

Description
Trailhead. This trailhead is a wide spot in the road where you can back your trailer in and unload.

Trails and marking. The Sugar Creek Equestrian Trail is a network of looping horse trails that wind over various types of terrain and through a variety of tree types. These trails began in

1990 when a local group of riders became interested in having trail access for horse rides. These trails are WAGON friendly.

As with any horse trails in the national forests when logging is done, markers are sometimes lost. If you ride knowing that, you will do ok. Carry a GPS and/or a compass and be ready to backtrack to your last marker.

Nearest Services
Food, feed, fuel, and veterinary services in Boonville.

For Information
Cold Springs Ranger Station
P.O. Box 417, 2190 East Main
Booneville, AR 72927
479-675-3233
www.fs.fed.us/oonf/ouachita

Sylamore Horse Trails

Distance: 4 loops, each is a different length, total 90 miles.
Difficulty: Easy to moderate
Fees: None at this time
Type: Public, day-use, and overnight camping; multi-use
Facilities: None
Water: Ponds and streams available for horses
Terrain: Forested setting with some mountains
Trail Markers: Letters on Carsonite posts
Trail Maps: US Forest Service Office, Mountain View, AR
USGS Quadrangle Maps: Calico Rock, Boswell, North Fork
SE, Big Flat

Location
GPS Coordinates: N 36° 1.78 W 092° 12.67'

From Fifty-Six , AR (east of Marshall), go northwest on Hwy. 14 to Gunner Rd. (FR 1102). An equestrian trail sign is visible from the highway. Turn right and proceed on the gravel road 3 miles to Gunner Pool Recreation Area. Continue four more miles along FR 1102 and make a left turn on Tie Ridge Rd. Follow this .4 of a mile to the trailhead. Signs scattered along the way help guide you.

Description

Trailheads. The trailhead is a large open area with no facilities of any kinds except for a handicapped ramp. The nearest horse water is about a quarter of a mile in a pond.

Trails and marking. Hidden Springs (Loop A): This is the shortest loop, which is 10.1 miles in length. It offers easy terrain. At the watering hole you will find hitching posts so you can tie up and walk to a waterfall up the creek.

Sandy Flat Loop (Loop B): 13.9 miles long the sandy flat loop is easy and recommended for beginners. This loop travels around the Sylamore Experimental Forest. The majority of this loop consists of flat open roads.

White River (Loop C): White River loop is 35.4 miles long. This trail travels across ridges past vistas, and has creek crossings. Part of this loop passes through private property. Be respectful of land owners rights and privacy.

McGowan (Loop D): The McGowan Loop covers a total of 30 miles. The loop gets its name because it traverses McGowan Ridge. Some vistas on this loop give you a view of Missouri some twenty miles away.

Point of Interest

Mosquitoes can be bad at the campground at certain times of the year. Be sure to take some insect repellant. Most of the horse trail is located on maintained forest roads. Watch out for vehicle traffic and ATVs. Riders are asked to remove all hay and manure from designated camping and day-use areas. Check wildlife management area hunting seasons and use caution.

Nearest Services

Seven miles to Fifty-Six, AR for camping supplies. Nearest veterinary or hospital services are in Mountain View which is approximately 20 miles.

Information

U.S. Forest Service
P.O. Box 1279
Mountain View, AR 72560
870-269-3228
www.fs.fed.us/oonf/ozarks

Two Rivers Equestrian Trail

Distance: 4 miles
Difficulty: Easy
Fees: None
Type: Public, day-use
Facilities: None
Water: None
Terrain: Flat grassland, and pasture with some brush
Trail Markers: Painted signs at intersections
Trail Maps: None
USGS Quadrangle Map: Little Rock

Location GPS Coordinates: N 34° 48.792' W 092° 24.128 From Hwy 10 west of Little Rock, turn north on Pinnacle Valley Road. Follow this past a beautiful horse farm. When you see the sign Maumelle Park ignore it and follow the road straight ahead. You will see a sign Two Rivers. Drive around the community garden area and you will see the sign for designated parking on your left.

Description

Trailhead. The trailhead is a blacktop parking area with aluminum hitching rails.

Trails and marking. This urban trail begins under a large cottonwood tree near the trailhead. As you look at the sign it points down a row of trees. If you continue that way you will find yourself behind a small barn near a very large barking dog. Continue around the end of those trees and you will find a large open field on your right. A trail cuts across this pasture to the equestrian trail. You will also find a blacktop trail for runners, walkers, and bikers.

Riding near the river is fun. Not often you can ride where you see large boats moored to a home dock. The trails are flat and fast. They are also full of deer. Ride with a deep seat and be ready for some athletic action from your horse if a deer startles him in the deep brush near you.

Point of Interest

This is a great urban bridle trail with room to feel free. You don't hear the heavy traffic you hear on the trail at Burns Park. Wildlife is abundant and birders should love this place.

Nearest Services

Little Rock

For More Information

Parks and Recreation Department, City of Little Rock
Pulaski County

Village Creek Horse Trails

Distance: 15 miles
Difficulty: Easy
Fees: $5.00 for day use
Type: Public, day-use at this time
Facilities: None
Water: None
Terrain: Hilly with woods
Trail Markers: Markers at corners
Trail Maps: Yes, at the Visitors Center

Location
GPS Coordinates: N35°10.883' W090° 41.799'
Village Creek State Park is located 6 miles south of Wynne or 13 miles north of Forrest City. It is one hour out of Memphis and two hours out of Little Rock. Use Hwy 284.

Description
Trailhead. From the Visitors Center drive out the driveway and straight across the road. From there follow the blacktop and stay to the left. You will end in a large gravel parking lot. There is plenty of room for even the largest rigs.

Trails and marking. The trails are not marked on the trees and they really don't need to be. This trail has been hand cut and it is obvious where to ride. Each intersection is well marked so you know which trail you are on and which one goes back to camp.

Point of Interest
You do need to call in advance. These trails are on very special soil. Crowley's Ridge is not like any where else in Arkansas. Many of the trees are different and all of the land is different. You definitely ride some hogback ridges in this area and they are not formed of rock. Your animals do not need shoes on this trail. To protect the unique top soil the trail closes after hard rains. When you ride there you will understand why.

Be sure to bring your Coggins papers. You can't ride without them.

This is one of the newest trails in Arkansas. The campsite is not complete although it is in the plans. There is a campground that is used for special rides. You can call for these special ride dates.

Rules

* You must register at the Visitors Center.
* You must have your Coggins papers.
* Do not tie directly to trees.
* Place manure in designated areas.
* Horses are allowed on horse trails and in the parking area only.

Nearest Services

You will find food, fuel, and emergency services in Wynne and Forrest City.

For More Information

Village Creek State Park
201 CR 754
Wynne, AR 72396
870-238-9406
www.arkansasstateparks.com/parks/park.asp?id=21

Viles Branch Equestrian Trail

Distance: 20 miles
Difficulty: Easy to moderate
Fees: None at this time
Type: Public, day-use, and overnight camping
Facilities: None
Water: Ponds and streams available for horses
Terrain: Forested setting with some mountains
Trail Markers: Yellow and white rectangles painted on trees.
Trail Maps: Caddo Ranger District Office, Glenwood, AR
USGS Quadrangle Maps: Athens; Umpire

Location
GPS coordinates: N 34° 46.552' W 093° 51.273'

From Glenwood, take Highway 70 east to Salem, turn right on Highway 84 to Langley, then turn right on Highway 369. Travel 3 miles to FR2106. There will be a sign on the right, "Viles Branch Equestrian Trail", pointing toward the horse camp. Turn left and immediately cross a low water bridge. Follow this narrow gravel road for .4 of a mile.

Description

Trailhead. The wide-open space on the right is camp. This is a solid gravel base and a safe bottom even in wet weather. No shade. No water. You have to ride a quarter of a mile to the nearest horse water.

Trails and marking. To access the trail continue down the road you came in on. You will ride into a cul de sac and see the trail sign. The trail begins by weaving between two sections of a split rail fence. From this point on, the scenery just gets better. Most of the ride is single file trail with one or two steep climbs. The trail meanders up and down the creek banks and requires several crossings. These crossing run from cannon bone to belly deep depending on the amount of rain.

Point of Interest

If you ride this trail as a loop you will have to expect some road riding. According to the FS map it is about 11.8 miles across.

Riders who are "road-shunners" prefer an out and back. The scenery is worth the ride.

Nearest Services

The nearest ice, fuel, and groceries are at the crossroads where you turned off Hwy 84. The closest veterinarian or health services are in Glenwood.

For Information

Caddo Ranger District
101 Smokey Bear Lane
Glenwood, AR 71943
870-356-4186
www.fs.fed.us/oonf/ouachita

Arrowhead State Park Horse Trails

Distance: 25 miles
Difficulty: Easy
Fees: Yes, check with office
Type: Public, day-use and overnight camping
Facilities: Water, electric
Water: Yes, horse and people
Terrain: Rolling hills with trees
Trail Markers: Ribbons and some signs
Trail Maps: Yes, check at park office
USGS Quadrangle Maps: Longtown; Enterprise

Location
GPS Coordinates: N 35° 9.23' W 095° 37.70'
Off of US Hwy 69, 8 miles south of Eufaula; watch for signs.

Description
Trailhead. The trailhead is clean, well kept, and open. Most sites are back-ins. The trails begin right across the road.

Trails and marking. The trails are marked with ribbons. There are some signs but because of the way the trails are laid out next to the park roads, it is difficult to get lost. The trails are easy and pleasant.

Nearest Services
Feed, food, and fuel can be found in Eufaula.

For More Information
Arrowhead State Park
918-339-2204

www.travelok.com/parks
www.oklahomahorseonline.com/Trailride/oktrails.htm
www.oklahomaparks.com
arrowhd@cvok.net

Bell Cow Lake Horse Trails

Distance: Flat Rock Trail 5.9 miles one way,
  Red Bud Trail 12.7 miles one way
Difficulty: Easy
Fees: Yes, check with Lake Headquarters
Type: Public, day use and overnight camping
Facilities: Electric, restrooms with flush toilets, and hot showers
Water: Yes, for both people and horses.
Terrain: Open pasture, woods, and some rocks. Most of the trail parallels the lake shore.
Trail Markers: Trails are marked with paint on trees and ribbons. Be sure to look everywhere for the markers. The location of the markers varies with what is available to hold them.
Trail Maps: Yes, check with Lake Headquarters.
USGS Quadrangle Maps: Tryson South; Chandler

Location
Follow Hwy. 18 north out of Chandler and cross over the Turner Turnpike. A green and white sign directs you to the left on a blacktop road. You will come to a wide swinging curve. Don't follow the curve to your right unless you want to go to the headquarters first. Straight ahead on the gravel road takes you to horse camp.

Descriptions
Trailhead. The trailhead is open, spacious, and well kept. You will find large pull-throughs with some shade and all have picket poles. Most have electric and water. Two trails leave camp; one on the east and one on the west.

Trails and marking. Flat Rock Trail goes west. You can expect to see some huge eagle nests in trees off the shore. The Red Bud Trail goes east. The trails are single track most of the way marked with orange blazes on trees. On the Red Bud Trail you begin by circling down through some slab rock near the lake. As you come out of this section you will be facing a fence. Cross the road, go through a gate, and continue near the blacktop for about a quarter of mile. Some of the trees along this stretch are marked with paint to let you know you are in the right place. The trail is well cared for and maintained. Lost Creek has a neat crossing that shows the creativity and effort of the trail builders.

At point B, after rounding one end of the lake, you will find more restrooms, and a place to picnic.

This set of trails is located between Oklahoma City and Tulsa just off the Turner Turnpike. This is not only a great place for a day ride, but it is also a good stopover for long distance travelers.

Point of Interest

Although the commercial dreams of the early town leaders never came into being, the county did prosper in the number of horse thieves. William Tilghman, a premier lawman from Dodge City, Kansas was elected sheriff of Lincoln County and during his first thirty days, he was handed nine warrants, each for the arrest of a horse thief. He arrested eight of the desperados and recovered the horse in the ninth case. In more recent history Old Route 66 adds its charm to Chandler—a must see town, built around the old time square with lots of interesting small stores that beg you to stop and shop.

Camp Rules and Responsibilities
   * Do not tie horses to trees
   * Be sure to stay on the trail
   * No loose or hobbled horses

Nearest Services

Gas, groceries, feed or veterinary care can be found in Chandler.

For More Information

Bell Cow Lake Headquarters
1001 S. Steele
Chandler, OK 74834
405-258-3212
405-258-1460
www.wildlifedepartment.com/lakecontact.htm
www.oklahomahorseonline.com/Trailride/oktrails.htm

Billy Creek Trails

Distance: 8 mile loop to top of Winding Stair Mountain, 10 or 7 mile loop if you ride to Horse Thief Springs

Difficulty: Moderate to difficult

Fees: Check sign in board. It will be a self-service pay station

Type: Public, day-use, and overnight camping

Facilities: Water and toilet within walking distance at the Billy Creek trailhead.

Water: None on the site at Billy Creek campground. Horses may be watered at the creek about a quarter of mile down the road. People water can be found at the RV campground within walking distance.

Terrain: Rough and rugged

Trail Markers: White and yellow rectangles on trees

Trail Maps: Yes, contact District Ranger Office

USGS Quadrangle Maps: Leflore SE; Muse: Whitesboro

Location
GPS Coordinates: N 34° 41.453' W 094° 43.89

Billy Creek Campground is located 2.5 miles north of Hwy 63, accessed by a gravel road. Approximately 5 miles west of Big Cedar off of Highway 63 turn right on blacktop road 6022. Horse trailers should follow 6020B after you cross the low water bridge. The parking area can accommodate 10 trailers.

Description

Trailhead. The trailhead is open and flat. The center area is divided into lanes or sites with long poles. The poles are simply put there to make you line up trailers. No haphazard parking here.

Trail and marking. Markings are yellow and white rectangles blazed on trees. The trail is mountainous, wooded, and steep in places. It climbs to the top of Winding Stair Mountain where you can turn left to Horse Thief Springs or right toward Winding Stair Campground. You may not enter the campground with horses. But if you pay attention you can ride around the base of the camp and hook up with the trail #7 that goes into Cedar Lake Campground. Any way you look at it you can ride to the top and loop back to Billy Creek. That is what most folks choose to do; trailer to Billy Creek for a day ride and camp at Cedar Lake campground where you have more amenities. The trail is beautiful and gives you wonderful views.

Point of Interest

Part of this trail is located on a turn-of-the-century logging trail. In the 1930's, CCC crews used this route to access Talimena Scenic Byway work sites.

Nearest Services

Sometimes you can get fuel at Big Cedar. I wouldn't count on diesel. Hodgen is closest for fuel and snacks. You can get groceries and other services at Heavener, OK or Mena, AR.

For More Information

Choctaw Ranger District
HC 64, Box 3467
Heavener, OK 74937
918-653-299
www.fs.fed.us/oonf/ouachita.htm
www.oklahomahorseonline.com/Trailride/oktrails.htm

Black Kettle National Grasslands

Distance: Unlimited
Difficulty: Easy to moderate
Fees: None
Type: Public, day use; in some areas you may camp overnight
Facilities: None
Water: Ponds and streams may be available for horses; in dry weather you may have to find a windmill. No people water.
Terrain: Grass land pasture, low hills, steep gullies; some trees
Trail Markers: None
Trail Maps: None

Location
GPS Coordinates: N 35° 36.85' W 099° 41.21'

To access the National Grasslands near Cheyenne, OK take Exit 20 off I-40 at Sayre. Follow U.S. 283 north 28 miles to Cheyenne. Turn west on S. H. 47 to a sign that indicates Battle of the Washita. The office is near the corner on the right. Pick up maps and instructions here.

Description

Trailhead. There is no trailhead as such. Your trailhead will be where you choose to park your trailer. You will find no facilities or water unless you happen to park at a windmill. Check with the main office in Cheyenne for a good place to start.

Trails and marking. There are no marking on this land. You ride on your own using existing roads and cattle trails or you ride cross country. Leave all gates as you find them.

The Black Kettle National Grasslands are managed by the U.S. Department of Agriculture-Forest Service as part of the National Forest system. This system covers 31,301 acres near Cheyenne, Oklahoma, and Canadian, Texas. They are managed to promote development of grasslands and for outdoor recreation, domestic livestock forage, water, and wildlife under the multiple-use principles.

Most, if not all, the Black Kettle Grassland is open for horseback riding. You won't find marked trails but you won't be riding in deep valleys or mountain sides covered in trees either, so getting lost should not be that big of a problem. The hills are bright red and stubby compared to Arkansas and eastern Oklahoma but they have a magnetism all their own. The Black Kettle Grassland is a checker board pattern which might create a problem for those trail riders used to riding several hours at one time. However, the country is beautiful and the land intriguing.

The Ranger who oversees the area indicated that some of the land is fenced because it was collected by the government for tax delinquent farms. When you ride in the area leave gates like you find them. If you choose to ride in the grassland, be sure when you ask for directions to the best area for riding, ALSO ask for specific information on where you can park your trailer. That was the part I found the hardest. I could find grassland but I often couldn't find any place for my trailer.

The ranger recommended Unit 66 for starters. You may purchase a map of the area. The office is open Monday through Friday 8 to 4:30.

Point of Interest

These prairie lands were originally settled under Homestead laws. Farming was successful for a few years but poor farming practices combined with strong winds and prolonged drought encouraged what became known as the "great dust bowl". Families abandoned the worn-out farmsteads leaving the denuded land to the mercy of the rains. Water raced freely over the red earth gobbling up the last of the topsoil. With nothing to stop the rushing water giant gullies eroded the land. Local leaders turned to the Federal Government for help. Congress authorized the United States to purchase these lands under the Industrial Recovery Act of 1933. Soil Conservation Service began rehabilitation of the devastated lands. Grass, shrubs and trees were planted and grazing was restricted.

Much recovered, today these lands belong to you, the public. Even though the land is again grazed on a limited basis, recreation including horseback riding is encouraged. Hunters and fishermen take advantage of the abundant wildlife.

Nearest Services

Several small towns are scattered around near the grasslands. Because the grassland is scattered over such a wide area you will need to consult an Oklahoma map for the town nearest to the area where you plan to ride.

For More Information

The District Ranger's Office
Black Kettle National Grasslands
P.O. Box 266
Cheyenne, OK 73628
405-497-2143
www.travelok.com/parks
www.oklahomahorseonline.com/Trailride/oktrails.htm
www.fs.fed.us/grasslands/

Cedar Lake Equestrian Trails
See Winding Stair Equestrian Trails

Cherokee-Gruber Wildlife Management Area

Distance: 22,000 acres; set your own mileage
Difficulty: Easy
Fees: None
Type: Public; May not be used by equestrians from September through January (hunting seasons)
Facilities: Pit toilets
Water: For animals only-- in nearby stream
Terrain: Open pasture, woods, and some rocks
Trail Markers: Some markers on trees
Trail Maps: None
USGS Quadrangle Maps: Zeb; Qualls; Park Hill

Location
GPS Coordinates: N 35° 46. 18' W 095° 40.43'
From the Muskogee Turnpike take Hwy 62 east to the Midway Gas Station approximately 13 miles. You will see a sign announcing Cherokee Gruber Public Hunting Area. Turn south and continue a mile and a half. As you approach the area the road will curve around a mountain, the blacktop continues left and a gravel road leads to the camp area.

Description
Trailhead. Although you can unload to ride as soon as you enter the Cherokee Gruber management area the best camping spot is four miles down the gravel road. The campground is pretty obvious once you pass the two primitive toilets. There is lots of shade, plenty of elbow room, and a clear flowing stream nearby where you can water.

Trails and marking. The trails are not marked except for one. Most of the people learn the area by riding the roads and then they learn the wooded trails in between.

Because this area is made up of 22,000 acres there is a lot of trail to ride without riding the same trail several times. Personally, I like to ride this kind of trail. People who want to road ride will find enough of that to keep them happy, but there are miles of single track trail through the woods, open meadow, and along Green Leaf Creek. You can ride over to Round Mountain for lunch. That is the mountain that used to be used for artillery practice. It is an interesting place to visit. Of course wildlife is abundant in this area. If you ride quiet and ride early or at dusk you have a good chance to see lots of deer, as well as raccoon, bobcat, and squirrel.

Point of Interest

The area is closed to riding 5 months out of the year for the fall and winter hunting seasons.

And here's fair warning, the ticks here are plentiful, abundant, whatever word you want to use to say "too-darn-many". Bold, energetic, and persistent, these ticks pay little attention to any kind of repellant. The best time to ride in this area is before or after tick season when it is cold. Otherwise come prepared for tick picking, off of you and your animals.

Specific WLMA Rules and Responsibilities

* Do not tie horses to trees
* Be sure to stay on the trail
* No loose or hobbled horses
* Park in designated areas

Nearest Services

All services can be found in Muskogee or Tahlequah. Ice and picnic supplies can be found at the Midway service station where you turned off Hwy 62.

For More Information

Oklahoma Department of Wildlife Conservation
P.O. Box 53465
Oklahoma City OK 73105
405-521-2739
www.wildlifedepartment.com

Chickasaw National Recreation Horse Trail

Distance: 15 miles
Difficulty: Easy
Fees: None
Type: Public, day use
Facilities: None
Water: None
Terrain: Open pasture, some trees, woods, some rocks
Trail Markers: Some markers on trees, some piles of rocks, some not marked at all
USGS Quadrangle Maps: Dougherty; Sulphur South

Location
GPS Coordinates: N 34° 29.49' W 096° 59.99'

The trailhead is located west of Veterans Lake in the Chickasaw National Recreation Area. From Hwy 7 in the town of Sulphur take 12th street south to the recreation area entrance. Turn right on the first road and continue until you see a sign that says Veterans Lake and take another right. It is hard to tell when you are at the trailhead because there is not much there to indicate where to park. Parking is beside the road anywhere near the trailhead. Look to the left as you drive along behind the dam. When you see an iron gate across a trail, you are there.

Description

Trailhead. The road has been widened to make enough space for three or four trailers.

Trails and marking. The trails are marked with whatever was available. You will find ribbons in some places, rock cairns in others. The trails are natural and follow ridges, cross small valleys and follow along creek beds. Huge red cedars dot the open areas and give the trail an excuse to turn. Elm, cottonwood and oak are scattered through the valleys. Springs, streams and lakes – water has always been the attraction at Chickasaw National Recreation Area. Rock Creek makes no exception. Not only is it a watering place for your animal, it is a great place to wet your feet and cool off on a hot summer ride. The 15 miles of trail wind along one arm of the Lake of the Arbuckles.

Point of Interest

Proclaimed the land of the "smelly waters". Indians knew about the many mineral springs that bubbled from the earth in the vicinity of Sulphur long before a white man set foot in Oklahoma. But true to form, early white visitors to the area extolled the medicinal virtues of the sulfur-scented water and a town was born. By 1895, a store housed a post office and the community was called Sulphur Springs. Hotels and rooming houses blossomed to tend to the needs of the tourists who came to "take the waters". Bromide Springs was "nationally known as a sure cure for nervous diseases and stomach troubles". Bromide Springs has since dried up but Pavilion and Black Sulphur Springs are still flowing strong near the park's entrance.

Nearest Services

All services can be found in Sulphur.

For More Information

Superintendent, Chickasaw National Recreation Area
PO Box 201
Sulphur, OK 73068
www.nps.gov/chic/index/htm
www.oklahomahorseonline.com/Trailride/oktrails.htm

Duncan Lake Equestrian Trails

Distance: 15-20 miles of trail
Difficulty: Easy to moderate
Fees: Minimal, check with management
Type: Public, day use, and overnight camping
Facilities: Electric, water, hot showers, restrooms
Water: Yes, people and horses
Terrain: Lake shore, up land pasture, rolling hills, some trees, some bogs if you get too close to the lake
Trail Markers: Minimal, some ribbons, some signs if you know where to look
Trail Maps: None
USGS Quadrangle Maps: Hope

Location
GPS Coordinates: N 34° 31.567' W 097° 48.848'

From Wynnewood exit off I-35 follow Hwy 29 west to Bray. When you see the Bray sign slow down and begin to look for the Duncan Lake sign and Duncan Lake Road. These signs are small and on the left. Turn left and travel 7.5 miles.

Description
Trailhead. When you reach the Lake you turn right into the campground. Drive until you approach a rock house that looks like the office. It's not. As you make a sharp right turn the campground is on your left. If you go down the hill toward the lake driving beside the rock house you will get to the office and boat dock. Some one down there will sell you an overnight permit. Equestrian sites are open, with plenty of room to turn large rigs. Some of the sites are more level than others. You may want to look around. You will find two electric hookups on each pole. There are some hitching racks, a wash bay and shade.

Trails and marking. The trail leaves the campground from both directions. One trail leaves near the restrooms. One leaves at the edge of camp on the west side. None of the trails are well marked but they are fairly easy to follow because they are well cared for and trimmed. Obviously they are used frequently because that is how we found our way around by following the used trails. There are some signs and some ribbons. None give you much guidance except where they tell you to stay out of the bogs. That was very helpful.

Point of Interest

I like these trails because they are open pasture, up land grass in most places. Of course you wind through some trees but for most of the time you don't feel really closed in. You get good views of the lake and on the south side you will find picnic tables under some trees by the old corrals. It is a fun ride. Trails wander around and you can pretty much get in as much riding as you wish. Explore and enjoy yourself.

Sitting on the cross-roads of the Chisholm Trail where cattle streamed north from Texas to Kansas, the town of Duncan is a great place to explore.

Nearest Services

All services can be found at Duncan, which is approximately seven miles.

For More Information

580-255-3644
www.travelok.com/parks
www.oklahomahorseonline.com/Trailride/oktrails.htm

Foss Lake Equestrian Trail

Distance: 14 miles
Difficulty: Easy
Fees: Yes, call for information
Type: Public, day use and overnight camping
Facilities: Electric, flush toilets, and hot showers
Water: Yes, for horses and people
Terrain: Trails parallel the lakeshore, some rolling hills, pasture and woods
Trail Markers: Mostly mowed with a brush hog, but may have some permanent markers
Trail Map: You will find a permanent one on the bulletin board or you can pick one up at the park office.
USGS Quadrangle Maps: Butler; Hammon

Location
GPS Coordinates: N 35° 33.198 W 099° 13.673'

Between Clinton and Elk City, OK take Exit 53 off of I-40. Proceed 7 miles north on Hwy. 44. At the intersection of Hwy. 44 & 73 you will see a gift shop on the right. This is also the park office. Stop here for current information. To get to the equestrian camp follow Hwy.73 to Mouse Creek campground. The entrance is on the right. As you pull into this area stay to your right. You will find a short loop that circles a locust grove. On the backside of the loop you will find the horse camp.

Description
Trailhead. The trailhead is a great overnight stopping area. I have used it several times traveling from Arkansas toward the west. All horse sites are back-ins but have plenty of room, plus water and electric. You may set up your corrals or use the picket poles.

Trails and marking. Trails are marked with some ribbons, but mostly by yearly mowing. Some permanent markers may exist now. Ride south and west to find the beginning of the trail.

Point of Interest

The high prairie that surrounds Foss Lake was formerly part of the Cheyenne-Arapaho Indian Reservation. Most of the land was settled during the famous land run of 1892. The land has been through booms, the dust bowl and depression, yet it still looks much the same today as it did years ago. Foss Lake was created by the construction of the world's largest earth dam, 134 feet high and 3 miles long. This dam blocks the Washita River and provides 8800 acres of water for recreation. Equestrian trails have been established along the shore.

Nearest Services

The nearest camping supplies, fuel, groceries and restaurants can be found at convenience stores along the lake front. Major services such as hospitals and veterinary are available in Clinton or Elk City.

For More Information

Foss State Park
HC 66 Box 111
Foss, OK 73647-9622
405-592-4433
www.lasr.net/idex.php
www.oklahomahorseonline.com/Trailride/oktrails.htm
www.swt.usace.army.mil

Hugo Lake Equestrian Trails

Distance: 10 miles
Difficulty: Easy, if it isn't rainy season
Fees: Check at the gate
Type: Public, day use and overnight camping
Facilities: Electric, water, restrooms, corrals
Water: Yes, people and horses
Terrain: Lake shore trails, trees, some bogs but only after rains
Trail Markers: Mowing and a few signs
Trail Maps: Check at the enter gate
USGS Quadrangle Maps: Hugo Dam; Ft Towson

Location
GPS Coordinates: N 34° 00.977 W 095° 24.636'

To find the Hugo Lake Equestrian Campground go three miles east of Hugo on Hwy. 70. Watch to your left you will see the Hugo Lake sign. Do not be confused by the WLMA sign which comes first. You must go past it. Keep looking to your left.

Description

Trailhead. The campground has lots of shade where nine back-in sites form a circle. The camping area is so near the lake, you can water on one edge if you choose. Each site has electric and water. Five sturdy metal corrals are available on a first come first serve basis.

Trails and marking. The trail takes off from the southeast corner of the camping area. It is marked mainly by mowing with a few signs.

Point of Interest

This is a Corp of Engineers trail. The area was well maintained and the trails were well trimmed and mowed at the time of this writing. Because these are lake trails you always have to be aware that bogs are possible after heavy rains.

Remnants of old Fort Towson are nearby. Hugo has its roots in the railroad. In the early 1900's more than 1000 residents were employed by the Frisco Lines. Hugo is probably best known for being the winter home of the Carson Barnes Circus. The cemetery for the Big Top is a special place to visit.

Nearest Services
All services in Hugo

For More Information
580-326-3345
www.swt.usace.army.mil
www.lasr.net/index.php
www.oklahomahorseonline.com/Trailride/oktrails.htm

Indian Nation Trail

Distance: 62 miles plus
Difficulty: Easy, moderate, difficult
Fees: Fees are applied by the campground you stay in
Type: Public, day use and overnight camping

Facilities: Depends on the campground you stay in. Cedar Lake campground has electric and water hookups. Billy Creek and Talimena are primitive for equestrians.
Water: Yes, see each trailhead for explanation
Terrain: Rough and wooded; lots of rocks with several creek crossings.
Trail Markers: Yellow squares nailed to trees, arrows pointing directions, and yellow blazes on trees
Trail Maps: Yes, contact the Forest Service
USGS Quadrangle Maps: Talihina; Blackjack Ridge; Leflore; Muse; Whitesboro

Location
GPS Coordinates:
Billy Creek: **N 34° 41.453' W 094° 43.898'**
Cedar Lake Camp: **N 34° 46.667' W 094° 41.885'**
Talimena Camp: **N 34° 47.020' W 094° 57.102'**

Billy Creek is west of Big Cedar, see **Billy Creek Trail**. Cedar Lake is south of Heavener, see **Winding Stairs Equestrian Trails**. Talimena State Park is west northwest of Talihina on Highway 271.

Description
Trailheads:

Talimena State Park is primitive camping for equestrians. Enter the park from Hwy 271 stay to your right and drive past the big rocks near the swings, turn onto the grass and drive toward the trees. You can camp anywhere in that area. To find the trail, leave the park past the restrooms. Follow that path until you reach a road. At the road turn left. If you are going to Cedar Lake, watch sharply to your left. You will find a turn very soon after a small water crossing. If you are riding to Billy Creek, follow the same instructions but watch closely to your right. Both turns are marked but you have to pay attention to see them.

Billy Creek Campground is flat and open you will find access off Hwy 63. See Billy Creek Trail. To find the INT leave the parking lot to your right. If you plan to circle clockwise and ride to Talimena you will cross a low water bridge and begin to look to your left. The INT takes off shortly past that bridge. If you are riding to Cedar Lake take the Billy Creek Trail which begins on the same road but farther on. The exit to Cedar Lake will be to your right.

Cedar Lake Campground is larger than either of the other camps. You will leave camp by accessing the circle trail that goes around the camp edge. Use trail 2 to 4C the INT takes off from the 4C loop in the Winding Stair Equestrian System.

Trails and marking. The INT is marked with yellow blazes on trees, as well as, yellow squares nailed to trees and yellow squares that say INT. You will usually find an arrow pointing the way at turns. Also look for double yellow stripes at turns.

This trail is not for beginners. You have to be thinking. You must pay attention. It is probably best ridden in one direction with someone to pick you up or to shuttle your vehicles. Otherwise it's a long trail a winding. This is also an excellent pack trail if you are so inclined. I would recommend scouting it ahead of time to be sure you can camp where water is available.

Point of Interest

The toughest leg of this trail is from Talimena to Billy Creek. It is tough because there are several serious climbs. Most of the trail is shaded but it is best ridden in cool weather. Anything above 90 degrees and you will stress you animals even if they are in good condition. Go in prepared for minor emergencies. If you know how to use a GPS carry one. If not, I highly recommend a map and compass. Prepare for the worst and hope for the best. The trail is great fun and a huge challenge. I hope you enjoy it as much as I did.

For More Information

Choctaw Ranger District
HC 64, Box 3467
Heavener, OK 74937
918-653-2991

www.fs.fed.us/oonf/ouachita.htm
www.oklahomahorseonline.com/Trailride/oktrails.htm

Lake Carl Blackwell Equestrian Trails

Distance: 35 miles
Difficulty: Easy
Fees: Check with the office.
Type: Public, day use and overnight camping
Facilities: Restrooms and showers
Water: Yes, for horses
Terrain: Open pasture and woods. Most of the trails parallel the lakeshore.
Trail Markers: Ribbons
Trail Map: Check with park office
USGS Quadrangle Maps: Orlando; Stillwater SW; Lake Carl Blackwell; Clearcreek

Location
GPS Coordinates: N 35° 33.51' W 097° 12.81'

Nine miles west of Stillwater on Hwy. 51, you will see the entrance. Turn north and follow the blacktop road to the interior. If you are unable to get a permit at the gate you will have to go on to the Lake Office. A permit is required for use of the primitive horse camp and trails.

Description

Trailhead. If no one is at the gate, go to the office to get your permit and they will tell you the shortest way to the trailhead. Across the road from the equestrian campground you will find restrooms with hot showers. To access the trails, cross the road and follow the ditch or trail that heads back the way you came in. Just around the corner you will see a rather narrow metal gate. Through the gate and you are on the trail.

Trails and marking. These are typical winding pasture, wooded trails. Most of the marking are ribbons. Good views and fun riding.

Point of Interest
You may purchase a yearly pass which will save money if you are a local and want to ride there frequently.

Stillwater, the nearest town to Lake Carl Blackwell, has roots that run deep into the history of Oklahoma. It was the location of the most ambitious effort of the Boomer's to grab and hold land in Indian Territory before the Run of 1889. A small lake at the north edge of town still carries the name Boomer Lake. One of Stillwater's first acts as an incorporated city was to sell bonds for an Agricultural and Mechanical College. This makes Oklahoma State University, one of the oldest universities in the state. Many students from the university and equestrians from Stillwater take advantage of the horse trails that have been developed around Lake Carl Blackwell.

Nearest Services
Fuel, groceries, feed and veterinary care can be found as close as Stillwater – just minutes away.

For More Information
Lake Carl Blackwell
405-372-5157
www.okstate.edu/oavpc/LCB
www.oklahomahorseonline.com/Trailride/oktrails.htm

Lake Murray Field Trial Area

Distance: This is an open area; how far you ride is up to you.
Difficulty: Easy
Fees: None
Type: Public, day use and overnight camping. Field Trials have priority
Facilities: Electric, flush toilets and showers
Water: Yes, horse and people
Terrain: Open pasture, some trees and woods. Some of the trail parallels the lakeshore
Trail Markers: None
Trail Map: None
USGS Quadrangle Maps: Ardmore West; Ardmore East Lake Murray

Location
GPS Coordinates: N 34° 70.22 W 097° 50.24'

From I-35 south of Ardmore take Exit #29 and travel east on U.S. Hwy. 70. Turn right on Scenic Highway 77, proceed about ¼ of a mile. The Park Office is on the right. Just beyond the Park Office driveway a sign announces Group Camp#2. Turn left and follow the blacktop for 2 miles. Before you get to the group camp you will see a large barn and dog kennels on your left. This is the designated parking and camping area for riders using the field trial trails.

Coming from the east follow Hwy. 70 to a four-way stop at the intersection of U.S. Hwy.70 and Scenic Hwy. 77. Turn left and follow the previous directions.

Description

Trailhead. The trailhead consists of a barn with inside and outside pens. If a dog trial is not in progress you may ride anywhere and you may also use electric. The trails begin right behind the barn, just follow the tracks.

Trails and marking. Trails here are not marked. You ride at your own risk of getting lost. Carry a GPS or get a good sighting on a landmark that can assure you come back to camp.

The Lake Murray trails are open and pretty. You can ride across pastures, through areas with scattered trees and, if you want, you can ride in the woods. The terrain is flat with a few rolling hills. From most of the hilltops you have a great view of the lake. The area is large and you are free to choose which direction you wish to ride.

Point of Interest

Lake Murray and Lake Murray State Park were named for the colorful governor, William H. "Alfalfa Bill" Murray. The state park is the largest in Oklahoma and was created in 1933. A 5,200 acre reservoir nestled in wooded, rolling hills is a peaceful place to regroup and catch your breath from the every day world. Yet for all its tranquility, this lake is the hub of recreational activity. The bird dog field trial event is only one of the many activities held in the area. However, it is because of the field trials, that horsemen come. The section of land which has been set aside for the dog trials is primitive, quiet and full of trails.

Nearest Services

All necessary services can be found in Ardmore: veterinary, groceries, hospital, etc. Picnic supplies and ice can be found at the 4-way stop corner store.

For More Information

Park Office
405-223-4044
www.lasr.net/index.php
www.oklahomahorseonline.com/Trailride/oktrails.htm
www.oklahomaparks.com
murraystatepark@oklahomaparks.com

Lexington Wildlife Management Area

Distance: Unlimited
Difficulty: Easy
Fees: None
Type: Public, day-use
Facilities: None
Water: None
Terrain: Upland pasture, some woods
Trail Markers: Roads with cut across trails, no markings
Trail Maps: None
USGS Quadrangle Maps: Purcell; Eason

Location
GPS Coordinates: N 35° 5.070 W 097° 14.101'

From Lexington take Hwy 77 north for approximately five miles. When the highway makes a jog left toward Noble, you will see Slaughterville Rd on the right or going due east. Follow this road for about 5 ½ miles, you will pass a church on the left and the WLMA office will be on your right. Turn there and proceed across a cattle guard. In a short distance you will see a wide flat parking area with a trash barrel. This is the trailhead.

Description

Trailhead. The trailhead is a large parking lot on the right shortly after you pull into the area. The spot is primitive with one trash barrel.

Trails and marking. This is WLMA land, mostly upland pasture with some stickers and sand plum thickets. The trails are on seldom-used roads with single tracks that cut across from here to there. It's a good place to ride especially if you have a gaited horse and like to put the petal to the metal once in a while.

Point of Interest

Don't be surprised when you ride over a hill and see an Oklahoma State Penitentiary in the distance. The facility sits on the southeast corner of the WLMA. Also this land is closed during deer hunting season.

Nearest Services

Food, feed, and fuel can be found in Noble. Veterinary and hospital service are as close as Norman.

For More Information

Oklahoma Department of Wildlife Conservation
P.O. Box 53465
Oklahoma City, OK 73105
405-521-2739
www.oklahomahorseonline.com/Trailride/oktrails.htm
www.wildlifedepartment.com/lexington.htm

McGee Creek Natural Scenic Recreation Horse Trails

Distance: More than enough
Difficulty: Easy
Fees: None
Type: Private, day use and overnight camping
Terrain: Rough woods, unforgiving black jack oak; mostly two track trail around the rim of a canyon, then the area moves into a wildlife or wilderness area. Do not ride in closed areas.
Trail Markers: Multi-use trails show a black printing on yellow background of a rider, biker, and hiker. When the trails change to just hiker or hiker/biker you won't see the rider.
Trail Map: Available at the Headquarters where you check in
USGS Quadrangle Maps: Farris

Location
GPS Coordinates: N 34° 23.342 W 095° 49.583

From Antlers, Oklahoma, take Hwy. 3 west five miles. Turn north or right at the Centerpoint Grocery Store. At this turn you will see two state signs. One says continue straight ahead on Hwy. 3 to McGee State Park. Don't. The other sign says turn right and drive 13 miles to McGee Creek Recreation Area. The recreation area is where the horse trails are. As you approach the permit station you will see a privately owned equestrian campground on the left. These are the only facilities on this side of the lake.

Description
Trailhead. The trailers should be parked in a small private lot just before the Permit Station. All slots are back-ins and fairly narrow. The trail is found by riding down the road to the Permit Station and looking on the far

side. The trail begins over there.

Trails and marking. The beginning of the horse trail is behind the Office. When you come to the McGee Creek sign in front of the Office, turn right and follow the little road. Once you have passed the Ranger's house, look across the road. You will see information boards where the trail begins. The trail is well marked at intersections.

The North and South Rim trails run along the crest of Bugaboo Canyon. Spaces in the black jack oaks let you see the horizon miles away. In many sections the rocks aren't bad so it can be a fun place for an easy canter.

Point of Interest

The black top access road to this recreation area is rough and spongy. Pot holes will shake up your horses if you don't slow down.

You can see the permit office from the equestrian camp. It is just down the road on the right. A person or group must get a permit to enter the area.

The land in the natural scenic recreation area near McGee State Park has been preserved much as it was when the first riders saw it. The 8,900 acres which has been set aside has four specific concepts: a quiet water zone, a wilderness-type recreation experience, non-motorized activities, and preservation of natural and cultural resources.

Trail Rules and Regulations

* Stay on the trails.
* Travel at a safe speed.
* Slow to a walk when approaching or overtaking other trail users.
* Walking, trotting, and slow cantering are appropriate on the horse trails.
* Horses have the right-of-way over all other users
* Do not ride on the trail when it is muddy. Deep hoof ruts are difficult to repair and make the trail hazardous for other users.
* Horses may not be tethered to trees or structures.

Nearest Services

Groceries, feed, veterinary and health care can be found in Antlers approximately 18 miles away. Picnic supplies can be purchased at the Centerpoint Grocery on Hwy 3.

For more information

405-889-5822
www.lasr.net/index.php
www.usbr.gov/dataweb/html/mcgeecreek/mcgeecreek.html
www.oklahomahorseonline.com/Trailride/oktrails.htm

Okmulgee Wildlife Management Area

Distance: 25 miles marked
Difficulty: Easy
Fees: None
Type: Most of the time this area is day use. You may camp overnight with permission of the local Ranger.
Facilities: None
Water: Horse water from ponds and streams
Terrain: Open pasture, woods, few rocks
Trail markers: Some markers on trees
Trail Map: None
USGS Quadrangle Maps: Nuyaka; Beggs

Location
GPS Coordinates: N 35° 37.83 W 096° 30.41'
The trailhead is located west of Okmulgee, north of Hwy 56. Once you are on Hwy 56 follow the signs to the wildlife management headquarters which is six miles past the Git-n-Go. Pass the Okmulgee Lake turnoff, pass the spillway; right after the spillway on your right is a dirt road with a cattle guard and a brown sign stating, "Okmulgee GMA". Turn right and go up the hill. You will see the headquarters; if you have a large trailer it is better to stop out by the big tree. Walk in to ask for information. There isn't much room for turning trailers around inside the compound.

Description
Trailhead. The trailhead is where the Ranger tells you to park. Check with the Ranger about where the actual trail begins.

Trails and marking. Marked with ribbons. This trail was laid out for the Cougar Prowl Endurance ride. You will find many sections that are not only beautiful but fun, because you can canter for long distances without fighting rocks. It is flat and what this author calls a "fast track". The best part of the trail follows the Deep Fork River in some big bottomland hardwoods. These trees will make you stop and take another look. You can also ride two ridges, one gives a view of Okmulgee, and the other lets you see Okmulgee Lake.

Point of Interest
The Okmulgee area has a history typical of many Oklahoma areas. It consists of Native Americans and oil. Okmulgee's history began after the Creek tribal lands ceased to be held in communal ownership and the Creek Nation was opened to settlement. A ride through this wildlife management area gives you a feeling of why this land was special to the Creek Indians who lived there.

Trail Rules and Responsibilities
   * Do not tie horses to trees
   * Be sure to stay on the trail
   * No loose or hobbled horses
   * Park in designated areas
   * All rules for riding in WLMA apply

Nearest Services
All services can be found in Okmulgee which is approximately seven miles.

For More Information
Oklahoma Department of Wildlife Conservation
P.O. Box 53465
Oklahoma City, OK 73105
405-521-2739
www.wildlifedepartment.com/Okmulgee.htm
www.oklahomahorseonline.com/Trailride/oktrails.htm

Platter Flats Equestrian Trail

Distance: 23 miles
Difficulty: Easy
Fees: Yes, for camping
Type: Public, day use and
overnight camping
Facilities: Electric,
water, restrooms,
shower
Water: Yes, people and
horses
Terrain: Lake shore, woods, single track and four-wheel
trails
Trail markers: Ribbons
Trail map: Yes, but it isn't effective
USGS Quadrangle Maps: Denison Dam 1958

Location
GPS Coordinates: N 33° 55.317' W 096° 32.658

Platter Flats Equestrian Campground is located near Lake
Texhoma just outside of Platter (west of Durant). Turn north
off US 69 at the Platter sign. Drive four and one-half miles
and turn right. Go another two miles and you will see a left
turn into the park.

Description
Trailhead. The day-use area shows up almost as soon as you
enter the park. You can park on one side where there is an
open meadow. The trail begins right at the edge of the road.
To find overnight camping continue to the park gate. Pay a fee
and turn right almost immediately. The equestrian area is
down there in the trees. The camping area is tight for large
trailers. I don't recommend anything longer than 24 feet in
the box. The back-in areas are also narrow. You have to park
between railroad ties which can be difficult to see especially if
you pull in late in the evening.

Trail and markings. The trails begin just south of the
camping area. The day-use and camping start at the same
spot. Trails are fun to ride. Many of them safely traverse very

close to the lake shore. You have a variety of opportunities to see shore birds and watch boats as you ride.

Much of the trail is single track but as you get closer to the railroad trail you begin to pick up four-wheel destruction. Things sort of have a maze-look. If you continue to look for red ribbons or ones that are pink with black stripes they will pretty much keep you on track.

Point of Interest

Platter Flats and Lake Side trails hook together making this system have the potential for a long out and back. Lake Side is a primitive area on the north side of the lake near Kingston. Both sets of trails skim the lake shore and meet where one neck of water reaches back into the land. Sometimes when the water is high you can not cross here. From looking at the map it seems the larger percentage of trail lies on the Platter Flat side.

Nearest Service

Food, feed, fuel and emergency services can be found at Durant.

For more information

US Army Corp of Engineers
Denison TX
903-465-4990
www.swt.usace.army.mil
www.oklahomahorseonline.com/Trailride/oktrails.htm

Prague Lake Equestrian Trails

Distance: 20 miles
Difficulty: Easy
Fees: Yes, check with office
Type: Public, day use and overnight camping
Facilities: Electric, water, restrooms and hot showers
Water: Yes, horse and people
Terrain: Rolling hills, some trees, and open pasture
Trail Markers: Ribbons at this time
Trail Maps: None
USGS Quadrangle Maps: Arlington; Sparks

Location
GPS Coordinates: N 35° 31.347' W 096° 43.432

Use Exit #200 off I-40 east of Shawnee, OK. Go north seven miles to Prague. Turn left on Highway 62 west. Travel three miles to right turn. You will see a sign that says Prague Lake and points north. Watch your mileage; go two miles, and turn right again. You should be going back east. In one mile you will see the camp on the left.

Description
Trailhead: The campground is spacious with some shade. Big rigs are welcome. You can camp primitive or use the level pull-throughs with all the amenities. Camp is equestrian friendly. You may picket with tree savers or use your own corrals. The Ranger says there will be permanent corrals soon. Bag manure and leave it near the trash.

Trails and marking: The trails are marked with ribbons and permanent markers at intersections. The marking system is still in progress. Because the trails hairnet around the lake, be sure you have a fix on camp before you leave.

Like so many equestrian trails this is a jog through history. You will find an old homestead with a marker to let you know a little about the family that lived there. In other places you will find remains of dwellings. You make up your own history.

Point of Interest
This is a new set of trails to be added to the Oklahoma list. It needs riders who care and people to support it. Come ride. Be sure to sign in and be counted. We keep our trails by the numbers that use them. Be aware these are multi-use trails. But multi-use or not, during the week use is minimal. Go and enjoy yourself.

Nearest Services
All services can be found in Prague. Don't forget to stop and see the shrine. It is a national monument.

For More Information
Park Ranger
Prague Lake
Rt. 2, Box 232E
Prague, OK 74864
405-567-2805
www.oklahomahorseonline.com/Trailride/oktrails.htm

Pushmataha Wildlife Management Area

Distance: Unlimited
Difficulty: Easy
Fees: None at this time
Type: Public, day use and overnight camping
Facilities: None
Water: Ponds and stream for horses
Terrain: Forest, some rocks
Trail Markers: Street signs at intersections and trail beginnings; some ribbons
Trail Map: None
USGS Quadrangle Maps: Stanley; Clayton; Snow; Wildhorse

Location
GPS Coordinates: N 34° 32.399 W 095° 21.296
Two and one-half miles southwest of Clayton on Hwy 271, turn right and follow the blacktop to the entrance.

Description
Trailhead. The parking areas are plentiful and primitive. You will find plenty of shade but that is all. Most of the spots are open. You should not have too much trouble getting a reasonably long trailer in here.

Trails and marking. The trails are seldom-used old logging roads marked with various street signs. Single track trails cut across from one road to another. You will find around 19,000 acres for riding in the Pushmataha.

Point of Interest
This area is maintained for hunting. Don't expect to ride here during deer season.

Nearest Services

Food, fuel, feed and emergency services may be found in Clayton.

For More Information

www.wildlifedepartment.com/pushmataha.htm
www.oklahomahorseonline.com/Trailride/oktrails.htm

Robbers Cave Equestrian Trails

Distance: 50 miles of trail, the trails are loop type, all loops vary in length

Difficulty: Moderate to difficult

Fees: Check with Park Office

Type: Public, day use and overnight camping

Facilities: Electric, flush toilets, and hot showers

Water: Yes, horse and people

Terrain: Mountainous, rocky, lots of pine trees, creek crossings and beautiful mountain views

Trail Markers: Markers on trees

Trail Map: Available at Park Office

USGS Quadrangle Maps: Featherston; Quinton South

Location
GPS Coordinates: N 34° 59.27' W 095° 21.24

Robbers Cave State Park is located 5 miles north of Wilburton or 12 miles south of Quinton on Hwy. 2, in southeastern Oklahoma. The equestrian camp is on a paved park road, which parallels the highway on the west side. It is ½ mile north of the park café & swimming pool. Signs announcing Equestrian Camp mark the way.

Description

Trailhead. Robber's Cave trailhead is sunny with some shade. Many of the sites are back-ins. Some have electric. Water is available. The trails leave camp in both directions. One goes back in the woods and one crosses the highway fairly soon.

Trails and marking. Markers on trees. These trails are the oldest public horse trails in the state of Oklahoma and are maintained by the Oklahoma Equestrian Trail Riders Association. This group started early with an "adopt a section of the trail" plan. Certain riders are responsible for different sections of the trail. This seems to be working well. The camp facilities are good. The trails vary in difficulty. All trails are beautiful. Because the trails crisscross in some places it is easy to set up short or long rides.

Point of Interest

The legends of Robbers Cave began as early as the 1700's with French trappers who used the shelter to store their trade provisions. Later the area was used by the North and South during the Civil War. However, the most infamous user of this cave has to be Belle Starr.

Belle used the area caves to hide many of her ruthless friends who were continually sought by the law. Part of the James gang was besieged by U.S. Marshals in Robbers Cave for the better part of 2 days. One outlaw was killed and others were captured after they were smoked out. To Oklahoma trail riders, this cave is important because it is within the boundary of the oldest public marked horse trail in the state. The trail was established in 1980 and has been maintained by OETRA since 1982.

Nearest Services

Fuel, groceries, feed or veterinary care can be found as close as Wilburton, 5 miles.

For More Information

Robbers Cave State Park
PO Box 9
Wilburton, OK 74578
918-465-2565
www.oklahomahorseonline.com/Trailride/oktrails.htm
www.travelok.com/parks
www.oklahomaparks.com

Salt Plains Horse Trail

Distance: 8 miles
Difficulty: Easy
Fees: Yes, contact Park Office for current costs
Type: Public, day use and overnight camping
Facilities: Back-in gravel pads, hitching posts but not one per site, wash rack, hydrant, flush toilets in the RV campground.
Water: Yes, horse and people
Terrain: Flat, grassy, open; excellent for beginning riders
Trail Markers: Unknown at this time
Trail Map: You can see a permanent one on the campground bulletin board or check with the Park Office.
USGS Quadrangle Maps: Jet; Nash

Location
GPS coordinates: N 36° 45.15' W 098° 8.86
On State Highway 38, 8 miles north of Jet; easy access with good turn around space for large rigs

Description :
Trailhead. This is a wide open place with shade. Plenty of room to turn long trailers around. Access the trail across the road.

Trails and marking. Mostly marked by mowing and use. The trail is approximately 8 miles long; accessed by crossing State Highway 38. The multi-use trail requires riders to be alert for bikes. This is a flat, fast moving trail. Enjoy looking for wildlife and new bird sighting.

Point of interest
When you are not driving an Interstate, Salt Plains is a great stopover for traveling to Kansas or other points west. People

are friendly and it's a great place to exercise animals that have been in the trailer a long time.

The Salt Plains (not the riding area) is a perfectly flat expanse of mud and salt completely devoid of vegetation. These flats are awesome in their desolation. Seven miles long and three miles wide, this strip of white salt and mud gives Salt Plains its name. This is the only spot in the world where people can dig for the "hourglass" selenite crystals.

A national wildlife refuge borders the park and more than 250 species of birds migrate through these crossroads. Some of the most frequent species are eagles, sandhill cranes, and pelicans.

Nearest Services

Food, feed, fuel in Jet. Veterinary and hospital services can be found in Enid.

For Information

Great Salt Plains State Park
Route 1, Box 28
Jet OK 73749
580-626-4731
www.oklahomahorseonline.com/Trailride/oktrails.htm
www.travelok.com/parks
www.laser.net/index.php
www.greatsaltplains.com

Sandy Sanders Wildlife Management Area

Distance: Unlimited
Difficulty: Easy, moderate, difficult. Set your own difficulty level.
Fees: None
Type: Public, day use and overnight camping
Facilities: None
Water: Ponds or windmill for horses
Terrain: Grassland pasture, low hills, steep gullies and arroyos; a few low trees, an abundance of cactus.
Trail Markers: None
Trail Map: None
USGS Quadrangle Maps: Erick; Willow

Location
GPS Coordinates:
    East Gate: N 35°2.76' W 099° 46.03'
    West Gate: N 35°5.48' W 099° 54.31'

To get to Sandy Sanders WLMA (west gate) take Hwy 30 south from Erick. You will see a sign announcing the WLMA. The entrance is on the east side of the road. You will see an old cow shed, wind mill and stock tank. There is plenty of room to turn your rig around and plenty of room to get off the road while saddling up. There is a bulletin board with maps and rules.

To enter from Erick (east gate), at Main and Third St. go south on Main past 10th to E1250 Road and turn east. In about a mile you will turn south on N1750 Road. Travel four miles on a blacktop and another two miles on gravel. You will see the Sandy Sanders entrance sign.

Description
Trailheads. The west trailhead is an open lot with a windmill. I pulled through two gates to get away from the road.

The east trailhead is near the Ranger's house. There is a large barn and corrals which a rancher leases. Do not park so you block access to barns or corrals.

Trails and marking. The riding area is subject to all the rules that apply to riding on Oklahoma WLMA land. Sometimes you have to contact the individual biologists that oversee that particular area to get the final word on when you can ride there. Most of the time these areas are open for riding, except from September to January. The land is open except for a fence here and there. You can choose to ride the roads that network across the area or you can take off cross country riding cattle trails. Near the highway you have to be alert if you want avoid the cactus. I thought at first the cactus was going to take the pleasure out of the ride but as I got away from the highway the cactus began to diminish.

Point of Interest

The land looks like many western movies you have seen with cowboys in cow country. You ride up on hills and see Herefords dotting the landscape. You might expect to see the big Conestoga wagons lumbering across the plains in front of you. In some places grass was growing chest high on my mule. Ruth loved it because she could easily grab quick bites as we walked.

This land is made unique by the cattle trails that lead to rocky arroyos, short box canyons and springs. A combination of Louis L'Amour and Zane Grey, this country just seems to call to riders. There is just enough of the devil in it to keep it interesting.

Nearest Services

Sandy Sanders WLMA is sandwiched between Erick and Mangum. It depends on which side you come in from which town would be the closest. Either town can provide you with feed, food and gas.

For More Information

Oklahoma Department of Wildlife Conservation
1801 N. Lincoln
P.O. Box 53465
Oklahoma City, OK 73105
405- 521-2739
www.wildlifedepartment.com/sandy sanders.htm

Sportsman Lake Equestrian Trail

Distance: 15 miles, out and back with some different loops, you can not ride around the lake
Difficulty: Easy to moderate
Fees: Yes, check with Park Office
Type: Public, day use and overnight camping
Facilities: Electric, water, restrooms
Water: Yes, people at the camping plus ponds and streams available for horses
Terrain: Trees, woods, good single track trails. A variety of terrain with a couple of creek crossings
Trail Markers: Ribbons and squares or circles nailed on trees
Trail Map: Check with office
USGS Quadrangle Maps: Wewoka West; Wewoka East

Location
GPS Coordinates: N 35°13.07' W 096° 33.15'
From Seminole take Hwy 9 east for four miles. Turn right at the Texaco store and continue for two miles. Turn left on EW 124 at the Sportsman's Lake sign. Follow this blacktop a mile or so, and then cross a cattle guard. Take the first left on a gravel road. Follow the signs to the day-use parking area.

Description
Trailhead. Overnight camping is across the road from the day use parking lot. Access the trail from the day-use lot.
Trails and marking. Markings on trees. Sportsman's Lake trails are diverse, ranging in difficulty from very easy to challenging. The trail traverses rough rock outcroppings and passes through small quiet valleys. Creek crossings provide water breaks for the horses. Midway through the ride a picnic table waits under a big shade tree. The table and benches were provided by the Oklahoma Equestrian Trail Riders Association. Much of the trail is sandy but there is enough rock that shoes are highly recommended.

As is true on any trail, watch the creek crossings during wet weather.

Point of Interest

From a Mekusudy Indian Mission, to a settlement known as "Tidmore", to a population of over 35,000 during the oil boom, Seminole was a community with growing pains. Vice and corruption came with the oil boom. Bootlegging, hijacking, and brawling were common occurrences. But the city recovered from the problems associated with the development of the Greater Seminole Oil Field. Even though Fixico #1, which started it all, no longer pumps, a replica of the rig sits in the city Municipal Park. Horse trails throughout the area wander through or around vintage pieces of drilling equipment which leave us memories of the great boom times.

Nearest Services

Veterinary, gas, food, and feed and health care can be found in Seminole, approximately six miles. Picnic supplies can be found at the store on the corner of Hwy 9.

For more information

Sportsman Lake
Rt. 2, Box 194T
Seminole, OK 74868
405-257-3600
www.oklahomahorseonline.com/Trailride/oktrails.htm

Upper Kiamichi River Wilderness

Distance: 12 miles across; you can ride 22 plus if you hook up with the Equestrian 8 Trail in Arkansas.

Difficulty: Difficult

Fees: Check at the bulletin board in Horse Pen Campground. It is self-service for over-night camping.

Type: Public, day-use at both trailheads and overnight camping from Horse Pen trailhead

Facilities: None

Water: Creeks for horses

Terrain: Woody, mountainous, several creek crossings and ROCKS

Trail Markers: Blazes on trees

Trail Map: None

USGS Quadrangle Maps: Big Cedar; Page; Mt. Fork

Location
GPS Coordinates:
   Kiamichi N **34° 39.527' W 094° 35.950'**
   Horse Pen **N 34° 39.025' W 094° 28.110'**

There are two trailheads (one with a campground) in the Upper Kiamichi River Wilderness.

Pashubbe Trailhead is located off Hwy 259 just north Big Cedar. A large trailhead sign is on the east side of the highway where you turn. Follow this road until it ends at the trailhead. There is no camping; day parking for maybe only three trailers. Remember when you unload here you are on your own. You are not supposed to ride the Ouachita Trail but you may ride in the Wilderness.

Horse Pen Campground is located off Highway 63 on Forest Road 6044 almost at the Oklahoma/Arkansas border. It is on the north side of the highway. Once you leave the highway it is maybe a half mile down a Forest Road to camp. The camp is large and open; the horse trail begins behind the sign and heads up. There is plenty of parking here with lots of hitching rails. This is a great campground.

Description

Trailhead. The Pashubbe trailhead is a simple circle at the end of the road.

The Horse Pen trailhead is a clear, large, camping area with plenty of hitching rails. The trail leaves from behind the bulletin board.

Trails and marking. The markings are blazes on trees. This is a strenuous trail for both horse and rider. Your horse should be in good condition and you need shoes (an easy boot is good emergency gear). These rocks can grab your shoes before you know it.

Point of Interest

This trail can end at County Road 100 which will connect to the Equestrian 8 Trail in Arkansas. You can attach these trails for a good long ride. It would be good for packing or for shuttling your vehicles from one end to the other. However you ride this trail, it will be a challenge. Go prepared.

Nearest Services

All services can be found in Mena, AR.

For More Information

Choctaw Ranger District
52175 US Hwy 59
Hodgen, OK 74939-3145
918-653-2991

Kiamichi Ranger District
PO Box 577
Talihina, OK 74571
918-567-2326
www.fs.fed.us/oonf/ouachita.htm
www.recreation.gov
www.wilderness.net

Walker Creek Equestrian Trail

Distance: 13 miles
Difficulty: Easy
Fees: None at this time
Type: Public; day-use; multi-use
Facilities: None
Water: Ponds and streams available for horses
Terrain: Grassland setting with some mixed oak forest along creek bottoms; few, if any, rocks; three primitive creek crossings
Trail Markers: Bi-annual mowing and a few Carsonite markers or wooden posts
Trail Map: Yes, contact managing office
USGS Quadrangle Maps: Temple

Location
GPS Coordinates: N 34°18.56' W 098° 6.21'
From Waurika take Hwy 5 northwest to Corum Road. Turn right and follow the blacktop one mile past Wichita Ridge Park which is on the east side of the road. Look for a sign that states "Walker Creek Nature Trail". Trailhead parking will be on the right.

Description
Trailhead. The trailhead is well marked with a sign near the gate. You will find a large gravel lot with no shade. It does have a strong pipe fence which can be used as a hitching rack while saddling. This parking area is for day-use. If you want to spend the night call management and they have a pasture a half mile down the road that can be used on a limited basis.

Trails and marking. Turns and intersections are marked with Carsonite posts that have a rider, hiker and arrow indicating the direction of travel.

The ground is sandy and great for galloping. The trail winds through cottonwood and willow thickets that provide some shade. This is a tall grass prairie with some oaks scattered through it. Several sections of the trail are enhanced by sand plum bushes that provide a nice snack if you are there during the ripe season. Law enforcement patrols provide security for trailers. This trail is not open during deer season.

Point of Interest

With a name like Waurika meaning "good water" in Native American, it is not surprising to find a horse trail around a lake. This area has a long history for both cowboys and Indians. The main route of the Chisholm Trail passes within five miles of Waurika. Wranglers moving large cattle herds to the north chose this rich grassland to fatten their cattle during the drive.

The land, which was actually part of the Kiowa-Comanche reservation, was opened to white settlement by land lottery in 1901. The town still exploits it local pest the rattlesnake. Waurika hosts a rattlesnake hunt once a year when thousands come to comb the surrounding countryside for the scary, poisonous reptile.

Nearest Services

Food, feed, and fuel in Waurika

For Information

U.S. Army Corps of Engineers
Waurika Project Office
P.O. Box 29
Waurika, OK 73573
405-963-2111
www.swt.usace.army.mil
www.oklahomahorseonline.com/Trailride/oktrails.htm

Walnut Creek Equestrian Trail

Distance: 15 miles
Difficulty: Easy
Fees: Yes, check with Park Office

Type: Public, day use and overnight camping

Facilities: Electric, flush toilets, showers, level gravel sites
Water: Yes, horses and people
Terrain: Flat grasslands, some trees, lake shore forested hilly setting
Trail Markers: Ribbons
Trail Map: Yes, available from Camp Ranger or Camp Host
USGS Quadrangle Maps: New Prue; Avant SW

Location
GPS Coordinates: N 36°14.541' W 096° 16.900'
From Cimarron Turnpike 412/64 west of Sand Springs take the Hwy 209 West exit and go north 13 ½ miles. This is also known as Prue Road. The park is on your left. After you turn into the area, the Park Office will be on your left. Stay on this blacktop to Area 2, Section B for overnight camping.

Description
Trailhead. The camp is big, open and well maintained with plenty of room for large trailers. All sites are back-in.
Trails and marking. These trails have been found to be difficult to follow due to the lack of permanent marking but they have great scenic possibility. They are marked with some ribbons and by mowing.

Camp Rules and Responsibilities
* Do not tie horses to trees.
* Be sure to stay on marked trails.
* Bag manure and hay and take it home with you.
* No loose or hobbled horses.
* No horses in comfort station, shelter or picnic areas except for the designated horse areas.
* No riding on beaches.
* Be cautious of bogs in some areas.
* Stallions must be well mannered and double-tied.
* Generators in main camp will be turned off from 10 PM to 6 AM.
* No firearms or alcoholic beverages on trails.

Nearest Services
Food, feed, fuel and veterinary in Sand Springs.

For Information
Walnut Creek State Park
P.O. Box 26
Prue, OK 74060
918-242-3362
www.oklahomahorseonline.com/Trailride/oktrails.htm
www.oklahomaparks.com
walnutcreek@oklahomaparks.com

Will Rogers Country Centennial Trail

Distance: 18 miles, if you get to ride up Knights Hill
Difficulty: Easy, if it is not the wet season
Fees: Yes, check with Park Office
Type: Public, day use and overnight camping
Facilities: Restrooms and showers
Water: Yes, horse and people
Terrain: Grasslands, lakeshore, some trees
Trail Markers: Carsonite posts
Maps: Available on request when you check-in at the horse camp.
USGS Quadrangle Maps: Sageeyah; Oolagah: Foyil

Location
GPS Coordinates: N 36°27.90' W 095° 35.13'
From State Highway 88 near Oolagah, north of Tulsa, follow the Blue Creek Park signs.

Description
Trailhead. Primitive camping, but you may shower at the RV Park a half mile down the road. Although the rest of the campground is winterized on September 30 and reopened on April 1, the equestrian campground is available year-round.

Trails and marking. This trail is basically marked with Carsonite posts at the turns and intersections. The trail is easy to ride and uniquely interesting. However, it can be dangerous after high water. Some of the ground doesn't look boggy but it can be.

Point of Interest
Much of the recorded history of the Centennial Trail began in the early 1800's. Lt. Zebulon Pike followed the Arkansas River in 1810 and arrived in the Verdigris Valley somewhere in the vicinity of the Oologah Dam.

One of the first families to the area was Will Rogers' father, Clem V. Rogers, a blood citizen of the Cherokee Nation. Clem Rogers built his house at the foot of an oak-crowned sandstone bluff overlooking a vast expanse of river bottom. The house was moved a mile west of its original location to avoid its destruction when the water basin filled behind the new dam. This house is located on the Dog Iron Ranch and can be seen from many locations on the trail. Many of the towns in the vicinity have historical Indian names.

Construction of the trail began in 1975 and was a cooperative effort of the Corps of Engineers and volunteers of the Oklahoma Equestrian Trail Riders Association.

Nearest Services
Food, feed, fuel and veterinary in Claremore.

For Information
Oologah Resident Office
Corps of Engineers
Route 1, Box 1610
Oologah, OK 74053
918-443-2250
www.oklahomahorsconline.com/Trailride/oktrails.htm

Winding Stair Equestrian Trails

Distance: The trails are setup in loops so you may set your own length for each ride. There are 70 + miles of marked trails.

Difficulty: Each loop may be different according to the criteria mentioned below. See Terrain

Fees: Camping fees vary according to the type of campsite you choose. The more services you want, the more it costs.

Type: Public, day use and overnight camping

Facilities: 32 sites are reservable, 21 sites are first come first serve, 44 sites have both water and electric, 9 sites are non-hookups. Non-hookup sites have a central water location for several sites. Flush toilets and hot showers are also available.

Water: Yes, for both horses and people

Terrain: Forested, hilly with rocks. Trails are rated as easy, more difficult, and most difficult. The ratings reflect the degree of slope, roughness of footing, trail width, and how well vegetation has been cleared for ease of riding.

Trail Markers: Yellow rectangular blazes on trees.

Trail Maps: Yes, available at Cedar Lake Equestrian Campground and the Choctaw District Ranger's Office, Heavener, OK

USGS Quadrangle Maps: Red Oak; Leflore: Blackjack Ridge; Talihina; Muse: Albion; Whitesboro

Location
GPS Coordinates: N 34° 46.667' W 094° 41.885'

To find Cedar Lake Equestrian Camp drive 10 miles south of Heavener, OK on U.S. Hwy 270/59 to Holson Valley Road. As you drive toward Cedar Lake from Heavener, you will cross a valley and start up a hill. Somewhere near the bottom of this hill you will see a sign for a rifle range. Use this sign as a signal for your next turn. When you see a small brown and white sign for Cedar Lake turn right and continue 3 miles to the park. Turn right again and follow the signs to the equestrian area.

Description

Trailhead. The trailhead at Cedar Lake is large. The camp is laid out in loops. Some are closer to the showers and restrooms than others. The campground also has two handicapped accessible sites. Signs strategically placed around the Equestrian camping area show where to access the trails.

Trails and markings. Yellow rectangular blazes on trees mark the horse/mule trails. White blazes signify hiker's trails and blue is the Ouachita National Recreation Trail which is a "hooves-off" for equestrians. A trail circles the whole camp. This gives riders access to their parking pads without having to ride through the center of camp.

Post Mountain loop consists of trails 1 and 2 which is an 8 mile trip. The terrain is rolling with two creek crossing. The terrain is rated difficult.

Holson Valley is made up of trails 4, 4a, & 5. This is a 7.5 mile trip which offers a ride through the Homer L. Johnson WLMA. Ride quiet, this is a great place to see some wildlife. Rated more difficult.

Red Lick uses 5, 5a, & 6 for a 15 mile ride. This loop follows ridgelines overlooking the Red Lick Drainage. It makes two crossing over Cedar Creek and is rated more difficult.

Emerald Vista uses trails 6 & 7 to extend some distance. A 16.5 mile jaunt takes you over steep terrain with long grades. The ride takes you through both Red Lick and Shawnee Creek Drainages ending up near Winding Stair Campground which is closed to horses. You may tie up and use the facilities.

Blue Mountain takes trails 2 & 8 out 15.5 miles. This is a challenging ride that takes most of a day of consistent riding. The old fire tower makes a Kodak-moment out of a lunch break by providing a panoramic view of the surrounding valley. 2 is rate more difficult; 8 is rated most difficult.

Point of Interest

Everyone has special places they like to go on the Winding Stair Equestrian Trail system. Understanding that the thrill of discovery is part of the fun of riding trails, Horse Thief Springs, Billy Creek Trailhead and Peter Conser's House are three places you may want to discover.

Horse Thief Springs was first made famous by the outlaw Belle Starr, who lived near the small town of Porum, OK. Belle was known as a good judge of horse flesh and she coveted horses that belonged to other folks as much as she loved her own. Belle set up a series of stations 50 miles apart to exchange stolen horses from one area to another. Horses stolen in Texas were sold in Arkansas and horses stolen in Arkansas were moved to Texas. Horse Thief Springs was noted as one of the stopover watering holes.

The Billy Creek Trailhead is the farthest point south on the trail system. You can get to Billy Creek Trailhead from the Winding Stair Campground or Horse Thief Springs. Billy Creek provides access to the Cedar Lake Trail system for day-use riders coming from Hwy 63 out of Big Cedar. This camp is primitive. No facilities except hitching posts. The parking area is flat, level and will accommodate about 10 trailers. Potable water and restroom facilities are available across the road in the Billy Creek RV campground. Horses are not welcome there, however, a slot in the fence allows people to walk through.

A third point of interest to discover is Peter Conser's house. Although it might not be designated clearly on the map you can ride directly to this historic site. Only about 2 miles of the ride

 is on a lightly-traveled road, the rest is on trails. Peter Conser was a well-known Choctaw Lighthorseman who became a deputy sheriff of the Choctaw Nation at age 25. Later he became a captain in the Choctaw Lighthorse Mounted Police. In the 1820's these mounted police were sheriff, judge, jury and executioner for the Five Civilized Tribes. Prominent in the local business community, Conser owned and operated a farm, gristmill, general store, and sawmill. His 19th century house, now a museum, has been restored to reflect the family's wealth and social position.

Nearest Services

Fuel, groceries, feed or veterinary are 10 miles away at Heavener on U.S. Hwy 270/59.

For more information

Choctaw Ranger District
HC 64, Box 3467
Heavener, OK 74937
918-653-2991
www.fs.fed.us/oonf/ouachita.htm
www.oklahomahorseonline.com/Trailride/oktrails.htm

About the Authors

Both Betty Robinson and Pat Gordon are college professors by- trade, but long-time trail riders by-love. Betty is a freelance writer with articles regularly appearing in national mule and horse publications. Pat is a freelance photographer always looking for the picture to communicate a sense of place. They are both avid mule lovers.

"We dedicate this book to everyone who loves trail riding. See you on the trails."